Holy Cross,
Life-Giving Tree

For Graham,

with appreciation,

Donnel

Holy Cross, Life-Giving Tree

Donnel O'Flynn

With illustrations by Aidan O'Flynn

Church Publishing
NEW YORK

Church Publishing
19 East 34th Street
New York, NY 10016
www.churchpublishing.org

Cover image: "The New Creation, Opened by the Cross" inspired by Paul Gauckler's drawing "Sketch of the Floor Mosaic of the Byzantine-Era Baptistery at Oued Ramel, Tunisia" on page 43, created and © 2016 by Aidan O'Flynn and Jana Laxa.

Cover design by Jennifer Kopec, 2Pug Design

Typeset by Perfectype, Nashville, Tennessee

Library of Congress Cataloging-in-Publication Data

A record of this book is available from the Library of Congress.

ISBN-13: 978-0-8192-3367-7 (pbk.)
ISBN-13: 978-0-8192-3368-4 (ebook)

Printed in Canada

This book is dedicated to the unknown artists who created the objects depicted in these pages, and to the members of the Society of the Companions of the Holy Cross: eight hundred amazing women in whom the New Creation has taken root.

Contents

Introduction

This book began as a project that aspired to be a contribution to art history. It might have had a scholarly sounding title such as *Images of Paradise: Depictions of the Cross as the Tree of Life in the First Millennium*. Chapter two especially, with its commentary on a number of works of art, still shows many signs of having started out that way.

However over time my goal has changed existentially. I am not a professional art historian. Those who are, I realized, are already doing excellent work in their field without my input. What I have been for over thirty years is a parish priest. How I can contribute is by trying to help practicing Christians make sense of their faith—the very thing I have been about in my ministry. When I stumbled upon two important clues from Christian art history, I began to see how timely they could be for believers of today. These clues are that the theme of a New Creation is deeply rooted in tradition, and that the symbol of the Cross as a Life-Giving Tree is as well. I began to wonder: What is Christian life like when it is intentionally organized around that theme and that symbol? What did people who did this in the past really mean by it? What could Christian life be for us today, and in the future, if we did the same? Thus my project has turned into a different one. It is now a thought experiment about the Christian life and what it would be, if it were deliberately practiced beneath the Cross understood as the Life-Giving Tree.

Chapters five and six contain the provisional results of that thought experiment, and are the heart of the book. Readers could probably jump straight to them and get ideas for Christian living that I believe would be helpful. Taking Hildegard of Bingen as the guide, I propose that life in community with attention to the principle she called *viriditas* (green-ness) is a valuable way of intentionally organizing Christian life around the theme of a New Creation. I also propose that understanding the Cross as a Life-Giving Tree can bring peace, first among Christians, but also with others who do not share Christian faith.

But how did we get to this point? The theme of a New Creation is present in Scripture, as a perusal of Paul's letters will show. But it was not until I encountered it as a long-standing living reality in art and liturgy that I began to understand what a transcendent vision it truly offers. With the New Creation, the triumph of Easter and the empowerment of Pentecost go not just to the ends of the earth, but to the center of the universe. All things are new in Christ: that is the premise and the prom-ise of a Cross that has itself come to life, and that gives life. These are breathtaking horizons, and to claim them for Christianity requires proof.

This is why I urge readers not to skip to the end, but to go patiently through the first four chapters as well. Only then will the deep roots of the New Creation theme be seen for what they are—truly Christian. Those who work through the historical context (chapter one) and the imagery of ancient times (chapter two) will not only find how deeply present in tradition the Living Tree theme really is, they will begin to understand how it came to be and what it means. Those who meditate on the Scriptures behind the imagery (chapter three) and ponder liturgies that celebrate the Life-Giving Tree (chapter four) will enter directly into experiences of the New Creation that are alive both in the Bible and also in Eastern branches of Christianity still today.

I have left open the question of what the structures of life in a New Creation might ultimately be. A theme as organic as that of a Life-Giving Tree demands no less. My suggestions are only ways to open the con-versation, and are just a beginning. No one person can see all the ways that the Life-Giving Tree might bloom. Readers should therefore see this book as an invitation to a conversation, and to emergent development.

That is why the book has six chapters with discussion questions at the end of each. It is designed with study groups in mind—the traditional Lenten variety being the most likely. However, a study in the autumn would make sense too, in the context of Holy Cross Day, and so would an Eastertide reading. Whatever time of year readers spend with these chapters, and whether individually or in groups, my hope is that they will first develop an enthusiasm for the New Creation, and then find one another, to explore its promise in mutual encouragement.

Let me now introduce our protagonist and explain how I first met the Life-Giving Tree. It is indeed surprising to realize how extremely widespread depictions of the Cross identified as the Tree of Life once were. During the first millennium of Christianity, artists all across Eurasia and much of Africa created such depictions. Early examples can be found from Scotland to Tibet, from Ethiopia to the Caucasus, and from Rome to India. In these depictions, attributes of the Tree that God planted "in the midst of the garden" (Gen. 2:9) are given to the Cross of Christ. Flowers, leaves, vines, grapes, birds, and the four rivers of Eden adorn these crosses. The rich metaphor of paradise is applied to our most important Christian symbol.[1]

The implication of this imagery, I slowly realized, is that the Cross understood as the Life-Giving Tree was once a valuable support to evangelism and spiritual praxis virtually everywhere Christianity spread. A related discovery is equally intriguing: liturgy and art celebrating the Cross as the Tree of Life are still very much alive in Eastern and Oriental Orthodox churches. Indeed, the Eastern traditions appear to have preserved ways of honoring the Cross that go back to Late Antiquity.

If the Life-Giving Cross was such a valuable support to evangelism in the first millennium, it is natural to wonder if it could be of equal service in the third. The contemporary situation of Western Christianity

---

1. The Living Cross is not the only form of the cross from antiquity, but it is certainly among the more important, given its ubiquity. For other cross forms, see Jensen, *The Cross: History, Art, and Controversy.*

has been a cause of anxiety to many. We have seen a puzzling decline in overall vitality, especially in the mainline churches. There is persistent disagreement about the meaning of atonement, and the Cross itself has become a source of division and conflict. We could use some new thinking, especially if it is derived from such a proven source as the great missionary expansion of the first Christian millennium. I believe the Life-Giving Tree could well be a helpful resource as we seek to transcend our difficulties. Rediscovering its vocabulary and charm would give energy. It has an immediate appeal that should be attractive to the unchurched, as well as encouraging to those who already believe.

My encounter with the Life-Giving Cross came as an unexpected gift. It was when I learned about the Clergy Refresher Leave program of the Lilly Foundation that my journey began. Applicants to the program are invited to submit a project that "would make your heart sing." That is a very generous goal for a grant program! I wish to thank the Foundation for its kindness to me and to other clergy in need of refreshment, who have benefitted from some well-funded time off.

A footnote in a book about Celtic spirituality gave me the idea for my project proposal. It quoted an article by Hilary Richardson that suggests commonalities between the High Crosses of Ireland and the khachkars (cross stones) of Armenia.[2] My project proposal was to go and see for myself. My wife and I were actually able to do so in the summer of 2010, thanks to the Lilly Foundation, and it was a life-changing experience. High Crosses and khachkars are exquisite sermons in stone. However, seeing them in person convinced me of my ignorance. They were so different from what I was used to. What did they mean? Clearly both kinds of carving, even though more than a thousand years old, stemmed from well-developed iconographic systems, but ones I

---

2. Richardson, "Observations on Christian Art in Early Ireland, Georgia and Armenia." I later had the privilege of meeting Hilary Richardson in Dublin, and wish to honor both her adventurous spirit and her kindness to me.

did not understand. Asking questions, following leads, making false steps, and finding ever-so-many helpful guides along the way, eventually led me to the conclusion that a key source of the Living Tree iconography explored in this book was the liturgical and spiritual life of early Christian Jerusalem. There in the Holy City, a cult of the Cross grew up round the wood that was widely believed to be from Jesus's own cross. This wood, whose discovery was attributed to Constantine's mother, Helena, was safeguarded in the Church of the Holy Sepulcher. Encounters with this wood spurred the enthusiasm of pilgrims and the creativity of artists, who developed visual conventions to express Christianity understood as new creation. These conventions and images travelled far and wide.

Many of my guides in this inquiry are scholars of art history, and I want to acknowledge their remarkable profession. Historians of Christian art know a great deal about Christianity and even the atheists among them often understand Christian symbolism better than professional clergy. It is ironic to me that as the monks of the Middle Ages saved secular knowledge in the past, so professors of art history keep traditions of Christian symbolism alive today. I was so impressed by the profession that at first I set out to write an art history book about the Cross, but as explained above I did not ultimately do that. Working outside scholarly norms had advantages. I could roam freely, leaping blithely across academic disciplines and eras in quest of largeness of perspective. Nevertheless, I have always been determined to remain within the bounds of good scholarship. There is no point in speculating about things that just aren't so, when what is known is so deeply life-giving. In any event, I salute art historians, and wish them well. They have been very gracious and willing to share what they know, which has encouraged me to trust in the at-first-surprising vision of a verdant Cross giving life to the world.

I also especially wish to salute the Armenian Apostolic Church. Learning about this ancient Christian community and its fellow Oriental

Orthodox churches has been a delight.[3] It is a pity that these ancient churches are so little known to Western Christians, not least because they open a living window into early Christianity. Very early themes are still present in Oriental Orthodox worship, and offer a fresh perspective after all these years. Had I not by purest chance (or providence?) been present for the celebration of the Exaltation of the Holy Cross at St. Vartan Armenian Cathedral in Manhattan in 2009 and found my heart singing during the surprising liturgy for that festival which will be detailed in chapter four, none of the rest of my discoveries would have made sense. The metaphor of the Life-Giving Tree needs a living home, and the worship of the Oriental Orthodox provides exactly that. It is all the more remarkable when one considers that the Armenians were the first to suffer genocide in the twentieth century. They know grief and loss and nevertheless venerate a Cross that is a symbol of life. Happily, the Church in Armenia is reviving after seventy years of atheistic Soviet rule, and I salute its members for an unswerving focus on the gospel of a New Creation. They have been a constant inspiration in my quest to understand the Tree of Life.

Let me now lay out the plan of the book:

- Chapter one describes the context in which depictions of the Cross as Tree of Life were first created—roughly 330–630 CE, when the Holy Land was the spiritual center of an interconnected Christian world. It also discusses the particular factors leading to the invention of such imagery.
- Chapter two shows pictures of Life-Giving Tree imagery from the first millennium and tries to interpret their message.
- Chapter three lays out certain Scripture passages that are evoked by the imagery and reflects on their meaning.

---

3. The churches known collectively as the Oriental Orthodox are the Armenian, the Coptic, the Ethiopian, the Syrian Orthodox, and certain churches of India. Historically they have been linked because of a common refusal to accept the validity of the Council of Chalcedon, 451 CE.

- Chapter four explores the history of liturgical devotion to the Cross, and suggests ways for celebrating the Life-Giving Tree in worship today.
- Chapter five tries to anchor the metaphor of a Life-Giving Tree in daily experience using Hildegard's concept of *viriditas* as an organizing principle.
- Chapter six suggests ways the Life-Giving Tree could address contemporary conflicts of the Cross and also rejuvenate Christian praxis and evangelism.

This project has taken ten years to develop, during which many people with varied kinds of insight have generously guided me along the way. There are no doubt persons on the list below who will be surprised to see their names there, having long forgotten talking with me. However, I remember them, and in every case benefitted from their knowledge and interest. There are three categories: scholars, clergy, and others who have been encouraging. Among the scholars, I particularly wish to thank Robin Jensen for patient mentoring. Her book about the Cross is the most comprehensive one I know, and my desire to remain within the boundaries of her gold-standard scholarship is heartfelt. Among the clergy, I particularly wish to thank my former bishop, Skip Adams. His invitation to present my findings at a clergy day in Central New York was the first full-scale validation for the project I experienced, and opened the way to many interesting responses. Among others who have encouraged me, first of all is my wife, Janet, who has shared my travels, and persistently insisted that the Tree of Life story needs to be told. Without her nudging this book would never have been written.

Thank you then to:

Scholars

Peter Balakian, Tony Bartlett, Michelle Brown, J. Patout Burns, Susan Cerasano, Morgan Davies, John Fleming, Georgia Frank, Rachel Goshgarian, Peter Harbison, Peter Hawkins, Marilyn Heldman, Colum

Hourihane, Robin Jensen, Beatrice Kitzinger, Don Macgabhann, Vasileios Marinis, Barbara Newman, Danielle O'Donovan, Judy Oliver, Heather Pulliam, Hilary Richardson, Lynn Staley. I would also like to thank the Colgate University libraries for generous access to their holdings.

Clergy

Bishop Gladstone B. Adams III, Rabbi Dena Bodian, Fr. James Carlyle, Fr. Mardiros Chevian, Rev. Kate Day, Fr. Daniel Findikyan, Rev. Joan Fleming, Rev. Elizabeth Gillett, Rev. Ninon Hutchinson, Rev. Gay Clark Jennings, Fr. Karekin Kasparian, Rev. Judy Kessler, Fr. Gregory Matthews-Green, Rev. Jacqueline Schmitt, Bishop Humphrey Southern, Rev. Byron Stuhlman, Rev. Renee Tembeckjian.

Others Who Have Given Encouragement

Kent and Mae Bolstad, John Bowen, Milton Brasher-Cunningham, Christian Clough, Tony and Ceci Davison, Phoebe Griswold, Janis and Malcom Handte, Freida Jeffers, Kate Klein, Jim Krisher, Jana Laxa, Dianne Adams McDowell, Robert McFadden, Ariel Miller, Sara Ann Murray, Rose and John Novak, Sharon Pearson, Jeanette Renouf, Susan and David Rood, Alinda Stanley, the people of St. Thomas's Episcopal Church in Hamilton, New York, and Janet, Aidan, and Chase O'Flynn.

1

Context and Emergence

Cross so faithful, tree of all trees
glorious, having no peer;
such a tree no forest brought forth
with such blossom, leaf, and bud;
sweet the wood, with which sweet nails
its sweet burden undergoes.
—Venantius Fortunatus, "Pange, Lingua"[1]

It was in the first millennium of Christianity that the Cross of Christ began to be depicted and celebrated as the Tree of Life, that is, as a source of healing and growth amid a renewed creation. To be clear, such depictions were only one form of the Cross among many. Nevertheless, it was a prominent way of depicting the Cross, and although this tradition has been largely forgotten in Western Christian circles, it is still vibrant in Eastern branches of the faith. By taking a leaf both from antiquity and from the East, then, and learning about this deeply rooted tradition, we can find much to appreciate. The times seem right for Western Christian praxis to explore the possible ways this vision

---

1. Walsh and Husch, *One Hundred Latin Hymns*, 99–101.

of the Cross can come alive for us, which is the project for which this book will advocate.[2]

However, Tree of Life modes of depiction and celebration for the Cross originated in a setting quite different from our own: the milieu of ancient Christian Jerusalem. We are separated from that context by time and distance. Unless we bridge the gap, we will not understand how the identification of Cross and Tree originally came to be. We begin the book, then, with an effort at historical reconstruction.

Learning about the context in which the Life-Giving Tree came to be and the factors behind its emergence is interesting. However it can also be unsettling to our contemporary sensibilities. Many have become aware of the darker aspects of Christian history following the advent of Constantine: the very period in which the imagery we explore was first created. Furthermore, most moderns are dubious about the literal identifications of objects and locations with biblical history that was commonplace in those days. I would simply ask my readers to try to find ways to enter sympathetically into the unabashed enthusiasm the Christians of Late Antiquity felt for the Holy Land that fell into their laps when the empire became Christian. We do not need to endorse all the values of our forebears. However, unless we find the spirituality of ancient pilgrimage somehow intelligible, we will not understand how such an unexpected idea as a Life-Giving Cross could have become so widespread. Let us then set about exploring the long-distant period in which the imagery of a Life-Giving Tree first took root and began to bloom.

---

2. Two books published in the past decade that explore similar terrain (albeit in different ways) are Brock and Parker, *Saving Paradise: How Christianity Traded Love of This World for Crucifixion and Empire*, and Irvine, *The Cross and Creation in Liturgy and Art*. A recently published volume by Robin Jensen contains also many examples of Tree of Life themes: *The Cross: History, Art, and Controversy*. So much concurrent attention is noteworthy in its own right.

A Christian World

For three long centuries, from about 330 CE to about 630 CE, thanks to the immense power of a now-Christian empire, the Holy Land was a Christian preserve.[3] Brimming with sites connected with Jesus and with the Old Testament as well, the faithful found it to be full of marvels. Many Christians came on pilgrimage. Some of them stayed permanently to make the Holy Land a center of prayer, art, theology, and liturgy. To Christian pilgrims and residents alike the Holy Land was—I use the term advisedly, bearing in mind all that is to be said in this book about its uses—a paradise.

This is so different from the situation of today that it takes imagination to properly appreciate how easy it was for Christians to feel at home in the Holy Land. They believed it was part of God's plan that they should revel in its numinous accessibility. That the Caesars had become servants of Christ and had systematically opened the holy places of Christ to pilgrims seemed to ancient believers so miraculous that only divine providence could account for it. Today that same land is a contested space with multiple groups making divergent religious claims. Christian pilgrims of today must share the Holy Land with many who do not have their particular enthusiasms, and Christians who actually live in the Holy Land are now a distinct minority. However, for three hundred years Christians controlled the Holy Land. There was only one narrative of the sacred spaces and Christians owned it. In Late Antiquity Christians took full advantage of the opportunities this fascinating region presented for nurturing of faith, and the effects of their explorations are influential to this day.

The Holy Land was itself the spiritual center of a much wider Christian world. The gospel had travelled with surprising speed. Starting

---

3. The idea of the Holy Land is imprecise geographically. The basic concept is of those places in which events described in the Bible took place. For Christians, of course, this means places where Jesus was known to have been active—the Galilee region as well as Jerusalem and its surroundings.

from Jerusalem, as predicted in Acts 1:8, evangelists known and unknown carried their witness to the ends of the earth. By 600 CE, faith communities had emerged all the way from Ireland in the west to China in the east. In spite of doctrinal disagreements, which were important to the clergy and even to Christian rulers, at ground level the forms of Christian life were similar over great distances. Orders of ministry, the Scriptures, the sacraments, and the monastic impulse had more or less the same forms. Even the Nicene Creed was accepted essentially everywhere. A traveler could cross the whole of Eurasia, and parts of Africa as well, and find the faith lived in recognizable modes. A map showing the dates of the introduction of Christianity to selected sites makes the point.

Most of the dates are ascribed based on verifiable historical evidence. Some, like the date of 52 CE for India, rely on tradition: the group of

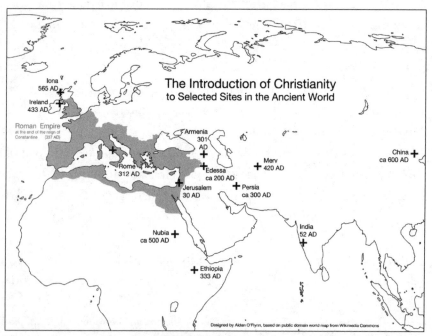

Medieval cartographers often placed Jerusalem at the center of the world, and this illustration shows how that made sense. The Holy City was accessible to Christian communities from Europe, Africa, and Asia. (Credit: Aidan O'Flynn)

Indian Christians known as the "Saint Thomas Christians" insist that the Apostle Thomas came in that year and preached in person. Whatever the source of the dating, it is remarkable to behold much of the entire known world touched by Christian faith. We tend to equate the Christian world with the Roman Empire, but in fact it was much larger.

This vast Christian world was interconnected. Peter Brown reminds us that "many divergent Christendoms . . . came to stretch along an immense arc" and that Western Europe was but "the far northwestern tip of that arc." Christian texts uncovered by archeologists, he says, are "like identifiable beads, found scattered from a single, broken necklace . . . texts that speak of basic Christian activities pursued from the Atlantic to the edge of China."[4] The Christian world was composed of a series of semiautonomous regions held together by a recognizably common pattern of religious observance. The church which took root in the Western Roman Empire was one such region—itself hosting distinctive sub-regions such as the churches of Ireland and Gaul. The church of the Greek-speaking East was another such region, and there were other "beads" as well: for example the Armenians to the East fashioned a distinctive Christian style for themselves, as did more remote communities in Ethiopia and India. Farther east still, the Nestorian Church of the East carried the gospel to China itself. Western Christians are often surprised when they realize the geographical extent of Eastern Christianity in the first millennium. Yet as Philip Jenkins notes, in 780 CE Catholicos Timothy of the Church of the East

> was arguably the most significant Christian spiritual leader of his day, much more influential than the Western Pope, in Rome, and on a par with the Orthodox patriarch in Constantinople. Perhaps a quarter of the world's Christians looked to Timothy as both spiritual and political head. At least as much as the Western Pope, he could claim to head the successor of the ancient apostolic church.[5]

---

4. Brown, *The Rise of Western Christendom*, 3–4.
5. Jenkins, *The Lost History of Christianity*, 6.

Two key factors keeping this vast Christian world interconnected were the development of the idea of the Holy Land, and the associated practice of pilgrimage to it. The Christian concept of the Holy Land—terrain where the feet of the Incarnate God had touched this earth—flowered after the Roman Empire became Christianized. Churches were built on the traditional sites of Bible stories while monastic communities sprang up nearby. News about the development of a network of accessible sites spread widely. Believers everywhere felt the lure of places Christ's presence had hallowed. On his distant isle of Iona, off the western coast of Scotland, Adomnán penned a widely read guide to the holy sites. He did not go himself, but based his work on travelers' accounts. To the east, the Armenian Church developed a great devotion to the Holy Places, sending an annual caravan of pilgrims to Jerusalem. A section of Jerusalem is called the Armenian Quarter to this day.

Those who could not visit in person devised ways to recreate the Jerusalem experience at home. In Rome, the apse mosaic at San Pudenziana church depicts the ascended and enthroned Christ seated before a city that is clearly intended to be Jerusalem. Its massive gold *crux gemmata* (gemmed cross) may echo one that by some early accounts was erected at Golgotha.[6] Similarly, the Irish High Crosses evoke themes from the Church of the Holy Sepulcher, according to Hilary Richardson.[7] In Ethiopia, the site of Lalibela is a

> mystical topography, a recreation of the holy city of Jerusalem. Eleven churches were carved from the living rock with a river flowing between them named *Yordanos,* after the river Jordan in Palestine. The names given to the churches . . . indicate the intention to create a new Jerusalem.[8]

---

6. Jensen, *The Cross: History, Art, and Controversy*, 100–102. Evidence for the existence of a gemmed cross at Golgotha is "uncertain but not inconceivable," according to Jensen.
7. Richardson and Scarry, *An Introduction to Irish High Crosses*, 24–26.
8. Grierson, "Dreaming of Jerusalem," 12–13.

Small-scale versions of the tomb of Christ sprang up across Western Europe, and to this day the English Church's Easter gardens bring the resurrection before the eyes of believers.[9]

Many of the faithful undertook the arduous work of pilgrimage in person, however. As soon as Constantine made it safe for Christians to live their faith openly, the flood began. The stream of pilgrims going to the Holy Land from all nations, and then returning home to tell fascinated audiences what they had seen and done, has been a feature of Christian life ever since. The flow has been interrupted at times, but never stopped for very long. The desire to see and touch and pray in the places Jesus walked and taught and died and rose again was as strong among his followers then as it is today.

There were a few dissenters—and prominent ones at that—who did not share the general enthusiasm for the pilgrim experience. Augustine in the West was curiously silent about pilgrimage, to an extent that is distinctive and has puzzled scholars.[10] Farther east, notes John Wilkinson,

> another strong criticism of pilgrimage . . . appeared in about 380 from the pen of Gregory of Nyssa: "If God's grace were more plentiful in the Jerusalem neighborhood than elsewhere, then its inhabitants would not make sin so much the fashion. But as it is there is no sort of filthy conduct that they do not practice—cheating, adultery, theft, idolatry, poisoning, quarreling, and murder are commonplace." Furthermore, Gregory adds, "We knew his incarnation by the Virgin before we saw Bethlehem, we believed in his resurrection from the dead before we saw his tomb."[11]

However those with positive feelings toward pilgrimage appear to have been in the majority. John Wilkinson has compiled and translated a number of early texts they left behind. Their journeys, by sea and land, lasted months and years. Detailed itineraries show them moving

---

9. Morris, *The Sepulchre of Christ and the Medieval West*, 58–67.
10. Bitton-Ashkelony, *Encountering the Sacred*, 38:106.
11. On Pilgrimages, PG 46.1009–16, cited from Wilkinson, *Egeria's Travels to the Holy Land*, 21–22.

methodically and with mounting excitement from one sacred site to the next, drawing ever closer to the all-important locations directly connected with Christ. Wilkinson notes:

> In this period the modern meaning of "pilgrimage" was expressed in Greek or Latin by the phrase to "go to pray" at a place. Prayer was thus the distinctive activity for the pilgrims in this book, and their goal was "the Holy Places" in the Holy City and the Holy Land.[12]

Some accounts of those who heeded the call to pilgrimage will help us feel what their experience was like, and also give a clearer notion of the context as a whole. One person who wanted to pray in the holy places was a woman named Paula. She was a wealthy Roman who visited the Holy Land under the mentorship of Jerome, who described her experiences in a letter to Eustochium, ca. 392/3 CE. Jerome tells us how Paula proceeded from Rome to Cyprus, and then arrived in Antioch. She then turned south, passing among other sights, "the Huts of Philip, and the chamber of the four virgins who prophesied . . . the place where Dorcas was brought back to life . . . and the house where the Lord made himself known to Cleophas," before arriving at Jerusalem where

> she chose a humble cell and started to go round visiting all the places with such burning enthusiasm that there was no taking her away from one unless she was hurrying on to another. She fell down and worshipped before the Cross as if she could see the Lord hanging on it. On entering the Tomb of the Resurrection she kissed the stone which the angel removed from the sepulcher door; then like a thirsty man who has waited long, and at last comes to water, she faithfully kissed the very shelf on which the Lord's body had been laid. Her tears and lamentations there are known to all Jerusalem— or rather to the Lord himself to whom she was praying.[13]

However it was another visitor, this one from Spain, who has left us our most complete account of the early pilgrim experience. A woman

---

12. Wilkinson, *Jerusalem Pilgrims before the Crusades*, 56.
13. Letter to Eustochium, cited from ibid, 81.

named Egeria travelled three years, and kept a careful diary of all she saw. Thanks to the network of Roman roads, she was able to see a great deal. As noted by John Wilkinson, she "must have visited all the places on the normal pilgrim round." This meant Jerusalem itself, Galilee, places near Neapolis, sites near Jerusalem—particularly Bethlehem and Bethel, and those to the south—in and around Hebron. She also made a side trip to Egypt. The places she visited "comprise three main types: first, there are the caves, 'houses,' and other buildings connected with the saints of the Old Testament and some connected with people mentioned in the New Testament; second there were 'martyria,' a word usually applied to the tombs of martyrs, biblical or more recent, . . . and thirdly the places of Christ's ministry."[14]

A charming account of her experience at Mt. Sinai gives a vivid sense of the highly developed Christian network already in place less than a century after Constantine. She writes:

> Pretty early on Sunday, we set off with the presbyter and monks who lived there to climb each of the mountains. . . . They are hard to climb. You do not go round and round them, spiraling up gently, but go straight at each one as if you were going up a wall, and straight down to the foot, till you reach the foot of the central mountain, Sinai itself. Here then, impelled by Christ our God and assisted by the prayers of the holy men who accompanied us, we made the great effort of the climb. It was quite impossible to ride up, but though I had to go on foot I was not conscious of the effort—in fact I hardly noticed it because, by God's will, I was seeing my hopes come true.
>
> So at ten o'clock we arrived on the summit of Sinai, the Mount of God where the Law was given, and the place where God's glory came down on the day when the mountain was smoking. The church which is now there is not impressive for its size (there is too little room on the summit), but it has a grace all its own. And when with God's help we had climbed right to the top and reached the door of this church, there was the presbyter, the one who is appointed

14. Wilkinson, *Egeria's Travels to the Holy Land*, 15.

to the church, coming to meet us from his cell. He was a healthy old man, a monk from his boyhood and an "ascetic" as they call it here—in fact just the man for the place. Several other presbyters met us too, and all the monks who lived near the mountain. . . .

All there is on the actual summit of the central mountain is the church and the cave of Holy Moses. No one lives there. So when the whole passage had been read to us from the Book of Moses (on the very spot!) we made the Offering in the usual way and received Communion. As we were coming out of church the presbyters of the place gave us "blessings," some fruits which grow on the mountain itself.[15]

Later Egeria's group also saw reputed locations of the cave where Elijah hid, the place where Aaron and the seventy elders stood, the burning bush out of which God spoke to Moses, the place the children of Israel had their camp while Moses was on the Mount, and the place where Moses became angry and broke the tablets of the Law.

We can be certain that Egeria's friends in Spain were riveted by her account. She was joined by many others from all across the Christian commonwealth who came to experience the Holy Land firsthand, and then shared what they had seen when they returned to their homes.

While there were any number of important sites to visit, for pilgrims seeking to walk in the steps of Jesus, nothing could compare to the Holy City itself. Jerusalem was the place where Jesus had taught, healed, been crucified, and was then raised from the dead. Paulinus of Nola (ca. 409 CE) wrote:

The principal motive which draws people to Jerusalem is the desire to see and touch the places where Christ was present in the body, and as a consequence to recite, "We will worship at the place where his feet stood. . . . Our religion prompts us to see the places to which Christ came."[16]

---

15. Egeria, 3.1–5.2, cited from ibid., 93.
16. Wilkinson, *Jerusalem Pilgrims before the Crusades*, 63.

Over and above this keenly felt awareness of Christ's physical presence, however, God's prevenient grace was also felt to be at work in Jerusalem. By a long-standing devotional tradition, Jerusalem was thought to be within the precincts of the Garden of Eden. Adam was said to have lived nearby and been buried at Golgotha.[17] Visitors to the Church of the Holy Sepulcher to this day are shown the reputed place of Adam's tomb. The Temple Mount was also frequently identified with Mount Moriah, on which the sacrifice of Isaac (almost) took place. These identifications long predate Christianity: Jewish thinkers were the first to make the connection of Jerusalem with Eden, a theme Christians were happy to elaborate in their turn.

To Christians, though, one of the most telling signs of God's continuing interest in Jerusalem was something negative, a feature that was *not* there: the Jewish temple. The structure so magnificently built in the time of Herod the Great had been destroyed only a few decades later. While suppressing the Jewish revolt in 70 CE, Roman legions burned and dismantled the temple complex, and left its grandiose walls in ruins. Christians easily saw this as the literal fulfillment of Jesus's prophecy that "not one stone will be left here upon another; all will be thrown down" (Matt. 24:2). When Christians came to power in Jerusalem, therefore, they deliberately left the Temple Mount in disrepair.[18] They did not build on it themselves because they valued the clear proof of the power of Jesus's words. Christian visitors needed but to lift their eyes to the hill of the Lord for proof of God's continuing judgment on the Old Covenant. The old way was in ruins, while the Christian sites were gleaming and new. As John Wilkinson puts it, "Christian theologians believed that Constantine had built nothing less than a new Temple, which eclipsed

---

17. Morris, *Sepulchre of Christ and the Medieval West*, 26–28.
18. Ironically, because Christians had deliberately left the Temple Mount vacant, Muslim conquerors later found it an ideal location for their own construction projects: the Dome of the Rock and the Al Aqsa mosque.

the glories of the ruined Jewish Temple, as they believed that the gospel of the Cross and resurrection eclipsed the old dispensation."[19]

Among the gleaming new Christian holy sites, pride of place went to this "New Temple" complex. The Church of the Holy Sepulcher, or the "Anastasis" as it is called by Eastern Churches, was built by Constantine to contain both the Rock of Golgotha and the tomb from which Christ arose. Its dedication in mid-September 335 CE was a grand event that was commemorated every year thereafter. A weeklong festival of the Dedication emerged and became the remote ancestor of modern Holy Cross Day, as will be explained further in chapter four. The festival of the Dedication drew great crowds. It was virtually equivalent to Holy Week in its importance.

Christian leaders—in particular Cyril, bishop of Jerusalem in the mid-fourth century—realized the liturgical potential of all the holy sites. They devised an annual liturgical calendar that commemorated events on the very sites in which they were said to have first occurred, on the particular days when they were being remembered. Thus Good Friday was kept at the traditional site of Golgotha, and Easter Day at the traditional site of the Tomb of Christ. The annual re-dedication ceremonies of the Church of the Holy Sepulcher were held on the anniversary of the reported finding of the True Cross. This scheme was as inevitable as it was irresistible. Anyone who has walked the Via Dolorosa today or been present for (or even seen video of) the New Fire of Easter will know the appeal. The very idea of keeping a "Holy Week," with different liturgies to commemorate its various stages, owes much to this early prototype. The worship forms developed in Jerusalem are the source of liturgies still in use today.

John Wilkinson points out that all this could be used as proof of the truth of Christianity:

> To Eusebius the [holy places] are holy first and foremost because they are visible witnesses to the truth of Biblical narrative. . . . Cyril of Jerusalem constantly appeals to the holy places as confirmation of his baptismal lectures: "Should you be disposed to doubt it

---

19. Wilkinson, *Jerusalem Pilgrims before the Crusades*, 61.

(the crucifixion) the very place which everyone can see proves you wrong, this blessed Golgotha . . . on which we are now assembled."[20]

To learn how strongly believers felt about the Holy City, which they felt was providentially within their control, we can turn to some verses written by Sophronius in about 614 CE. Sophronius later became the last patriarch of Jerusalem. To him fell the painful task of negotiating the surrender of the city to Arab conquerors in 638 CE. However the following verses were written at a time when the glories of the Holy City were still completely Christian. Believers felt this would be God's will for all time. Sophronius wrote these lines when he was absent from his beloved city, to express his yearning to return.

> Holy City of God,
> Jerusalem, how I long to stand
> even now at your gates,
> and go in, rejoicing!
>
> Let me walk thy pavements
> and go inside the Anastasis,
> where the King of All rose again,
> trampling down the power of death.
>
> Through the divine sanctuary
> I will penetrate the divine Tomb
> and with deep reverence
> will venerate that Rock. . .
>
> And as I venerate that worthy Tomb,
> surrounded by its conches
> and columns surmounted by golden lilies,
> I shall be overcome with joy.
>
> Let me pass on to the *Tristoon* [place of three colonades]
> all covered with pearls and gold,
> and go on into the lovely building
> of the Place of a Skull . . .

---

20. Wilkinson, *Egeria's Travels to the Holy Land*, 20.

And prostrate I will venerate
the Navel-point of the earth, that divine Rock
in which was fixed the Wood
which undid the curse of the tree.

How great thy glory, noble Rock, in which was fixed
the Cross, the Redemption of mankind!

Exultant let me go on to the place
where all of us
who belong to the people of God
venerate the glorious Wood of the Cross . . .

And let me go rejoicing
to the splendid sanctuary, the place
where the noble Empress Helena
found the divine Wood;[21]

Clearly the world in which Sophronius lived offered a rich context
for cultivation of the Christian life. He was fortunate in that he enjoyed
daily access to the most mesmerizing religious setting imaginable for
believers: Jerusalem itself, and places in it thought to be directly associated with Christ and further sanctified by centuries of liturgical and
artistic development, as well as by the prayers and devotion of countless
pilgrims. The experience of Sophronius, and others who actually lived
at the spiritual center of Christendom, was extended far and wide by the
mechanisms of cultural diffusion, especially pilgrimage.

Nevertheless, in the providence of God, the exclusive Christian hold
on the Holy Land proved not to be permanent after all. The Arab conquests that led to the loss of Jerusalem in 638 CE brought it to an unfore-
seen end. It is hard to know how to evaluate this loss. On the one hand, a
unique way of practicing the faith daily in the very places associated with
Christ ceased to be, and there was something to mourn in that reality.
On the other hand, the spread of the gospel did not come to an end. The
principle of Christ's universal presence—anywhere that two or three are

---

21. Anacreonticon 20, cited in Wilkinson, *Jerusalem Pilgrims before the Crusades*, 157–61.

gathered, not just in Jerusalem—was fully vindicated by the continuing expansion of the faith across the known world. In any event, many of the works of art we will consider postdate the conversion of Jerusalem into a stronghold of Islam. The Life-Giving Tree imagery that had flourished there continued to grow and spread its branches far and wide.

The Life-Giving Tree and Its Origins

We have explored the world in which depictions of the Cross as the Tree of Life first blossomed, between 330 and 630 CE. What factors led to their actual emergence in that setting?

One factor behind Living Tree imagery is that the connection between the Tree of Eden and the Cross of Christ had already been posited in theological writings of Church Fathers. Paul himself had prepared the way by creating a typology that contrasted the Old Adam and Christ the New Adam (1 Cor. 15:21). It was natural for theologians to expand this contrast in their writings, taking attributes of Adam's Eden, such as the Tree of Life, and applying them to the Cross of Christ. Writers such as Irenaeus, Tertullian, and Clement of Alexandria did precisely that, well before the time of Constantine. Whether rank and file believers paid much attention to these literary conceits, or were even in a position to read them, is uncertain given the low rates of literacy. Nevertheless, the identification of the Cross and the Tree of Life was indeed present as a concept from early times.

Given this fact, it is striking that artistic depictions of the theme seem not to have been created until after the time of Constantine and did not become truly widespread until later still. Possibly the first visual hint of the theme is the use of the four rivers of Paradise in conjunction with the rock of Eden/Golgotha, a trope that became widespread. Sarcophagi in Rome dated to 340–370 CE show this iconography. In these earliest depictions the figure of Jesus ascended stands on the Rock, from which the four rivers issue forth.[22] Other sarcophagi from the fifth century add

---

22. Jensen, *The Cross: History, Art, and Controversy*, 68-71.

peacocks, curling vines, birds, and flowers.[23] Most of the examples we will see are much later, dating from the sixth century and after. How then can we account for the difference in time between the emergence of a Tree of Life typology for the Cross in literature as opposed to its flowering in art?

Regarding the later arrival of Tree of Life imagery for the Cross, there are two key considerations. One is the great difference in the situation for Christians before and after 312 CE, the date Constantine became the first Christian emperor. Prior to that date Christianity was still officially proscribed in the Roman Empire, whereas afterward it enjoyed a clear official preference. The proscription necessarily had a retarding effect on the overall development of Christian art forms, whereas the official preference included widespread subsidization of Christian art and architecture. Official favor necessarily encouraged creativity and high quality work.[24] Second, images of the Cross itself were late coming on the scene. Prior to Constantine, crosses were rare, and when did they appear, it was almost always in veiled ways. Following his conversion, the emperor himself patronized cross imagery, giving it immense prestige.

These twin factors take some digesting for the modern Western Christian. To us, art and architecture are normal means of expressing our faith, and crosses are everywhere. We take for granted a rich universe of sign and symbol, but it was not always so. Apart from funerary art in the immediate vicinity of Rome and a few other scattered examples from further afield, there is very little positive evidence for early Christian artwork.

> Most of the earliest examples of Christian art are simple, almost humble, in their manner of presentation or choice of subjects. Early wall paintings in particular are almost sketchy and simply rendered, without a great deal of details or decorative elaboration.[25]

---

23. Ibid., 131.
24. For a comprehensive treatment of issues affecting Christian art before and after Constantine see Jensen, *Understanding Early Christian Art*, chapter one.
25. Ibid., 12.

Perhaps there was more art than we realize, and it has simply disappeared. On the other hand, perhaps not much Christian art was being created. The earliest believers tended not to be wealthy patrons of the arts, and they lived in a setting in which attracting outward attention was often not a prudent thing to do. Persecutions, though intermittent, were a reality always lurking in the back of the church's collective mind. An analogy in our own time is the agonizing decision faced by the leaders of Chinese congregations whether to accede to government demands to remove crosses from their churches.[26] Some Chinese pastors have cooperated by removing the crosses themselves, and others have resisted, only to have their crosses forcibly demolished. In either case, many churches are now without crosses and thus make less of an outer visual impression on unbelievers and on the faithful alike. A similar situation in antiquity must have been operative to retard overall artistic development.

After Constantine came to power in 312 CE, all this began to change. He soon gave Christianity a preferred status throughout the empire, and subsidized construction of Christian churches. Magnificent edifices were built and skilled artisans decorated them. Although many are suspicious and critical of the changes Constantine engendered, seeing them as the beginnings of militarization of Christianity, there are also things to be said in favor of them. Without his legalization and subsidization of Christianity, the symbols to be explored in this book might not exist at all.

This is especially true of the symbol that is at the heart of this study, the Cross. Today crosses are everywhere in Christian circles, but it was not so prior to Constantine. Depictions of the Cross from before his time are hard to find. Christians did indeed use the Cross symbolically as a gesture in rituals, tracing it on the forehead in baptism for instance, or crossing themselves to ward off evil.

---

26. See chapter six for a fuller discussion.

Thus, despite the importance of making the sign of the cross in everyday religious practice . . . early Christians did not—to any significant degree—incorporate plain crosses in their homes, tomb epitaphs, or even on small personal objects (rings, dishware, clothing). It would be the middle of the fourth century before crosses began to show up to any extent on such objects. Rather, these early believers favored devices like doves, anchors, or fish, which presumably alluded to the cross without actually depicting it.[27]

In reflecting on the reluctance of early Christians to use the Cross as a visual symbol, it helps to remember that crucifixion was still practiced in their times. Constantine ended the use of crucifixion. Before his unexpected advent, in days when it was still possible to see fellow believers put to death in the same manner as Christ had been executed, it is not surprising that Christians made but little use of the outer symbol of the Cross. After Constantine's accession to power, it would have been equally surprising if Christians did not begin to make use of the symbol of the Cross, since the emperor himself led the way.

The precise manner in which Constantine's conversion took place remains confusing and controversial, but we know that it included imagery of the Cross from the very beginning. His biographer Eusebius tells us that Constantine had a vision of a cross of light and a powerful dream about victory in battle in the sign of the Cross. Following this dream, says Eusebius, Constantine ordered goldsmiths and jewelers to make a copy of what he had seen in his dream. They created the "labarum," which became his personal standard and that of his armies. This device was a cross with a flag descending from the crossbar, topped by a Chi-Rho, the first two letters of the name of Christ.[28] Fighting under this standard, Constantine conquered his enemies on the field of battle.

---

27. Jensen, *The Cross: History, Art, and Controversy*, 44.
28. A Chi-Rho symbol was a common device in early Christianity, also called the "Christogram." It employs the first two letters in the Greek spelling of Christ. The chi has the shape of an "X" and the rho looks like a small letter "p." The rho is superimposed on the chi.

As sole emperor, Constantine continued to honor the sign of the Cross. A cross-shaped labarum is found on coinage dated to the mid 320s. When he built a palace in his new city of Constantinople, Eusebius reports, "The Emperor's soul was seized by such intense love of God, that in the most pre-eminent building of the imperial palace itself he affixed on a large panel in the center of the gilded ceiling the sign of the

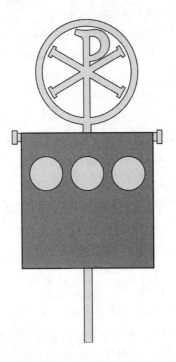

An artist's visualization of the military standard called the "Labarum" is based on Eusebius's description and also on a coin minted during Constantine's reign. It shows the intersecting Greek letters "chi" and "rho," the first two letters of the name of Christ in the form of a cross. The circles on the banner probably contained images of Constantine and two of his children. (Credit: Aidan O'Flynn)

Savior's Passion composed of various precious stones set in an abundance of gold. This, in his love of God, he regarded as the phylactery of his very empire." And for public display as well, "He represented for everyone to see upon a panel placed high aloft at the vestibule of the imperial palace . . . represented in painting the salutary symbol above his head."[29]

---

29. Mango, *The Art of the Byzantine Empire 312–1453*, 11, 15.

When seeking to account for the prominence of the Cross as a symbol of Christianity, therefore, we cannot overlook the importance of imperial patronage. The heir of the Caesars was well positioned to bring the Cross into prominence—out of the shadows and into the light of day—and his emergence as a Christian emperor made that happen.

To get a better feeling for the change in the overall situation of art following the conversion of Constantine, let us compare some works from before and after his day. Images from a catacomb in Rome from before the time Christianity became legal, make an instructive contrast to an apse mosaic in the same city created less than a century after Constantine. The early images are artistically simple, but they have an immediate appeal. The apse mosaic is a glorious and highly professional work of art and prominently features a magnificent golden cross. However, its very professionalism and the grandeur of its themes create a certain distance between the art and the viewer. How an ordinary Christian is to picture themselves as part of the scene is hard to know.

The catacomb images are photographs I took during our travels in 2010. They show reproductions on display at the catacombs of Domitilla, outside the walls of Rome. They recreate symbols found underground, deep within the perpetual cool of earth.

The combined Greek letters "chi" and "rho"—the first letters of the name of Christ—are flanked by the alpha and the omega, the first and last letters of the Greek alphabet, symbolizing the beginning and the end of all things. The letter "chi" is itself a veiled visual reference to the Cross because of its shape. Believers in that time would have easily understood the symbolism, but those who had not been initiated into the Christian way might have not seen it quite as easily. In this case the highly symbolic letters are embraced within a victor's wreath of laurel.

A figure in the "orans" position is at prayer, making the same gesture of petition and oblation as priests still do today. With his raised arms he may also suggest a cross-like shape.

A fish with the word **IXTHUS**—the Greek word for fish—is also an anagram, the first letters of the phrase, "Jesus Christ, Son of God, Savior."

A version of the Christogram as found on a reproduction from a Roman catacomb. (Credit: author.)

A dove with an olive branch recalls the salvation that Noah found after the Great Flood, and reminds the viewer that God's saving power is still available to humanity. It also suggests the dove of the Holy Spirit.

The Good Shepherd with a lost lamb safely borne upon his shoulders was a favorite image to early Christians. Like the dove of Noah, it underscores God's active power to protect and redeem in daily life.

The anchor is another veiled reference to the Cross. This anchor has caught two fish, symbolizing believers secured by Christ. This is as near a direct representation of the "salutary symbol" (to use Eusebius' term for the Cross quoted earlier) as one will find in the very early setting of the catacombs.

The contrasting illustration, demonstrating the new prominence of the Cross following the great changes wrought by Constantine, is the apse mosaic at San Pudenziana church in Rome.

It is the earliest such mosaic in any Roman church, dating to the papacy of Innocent I (402–417 CE)—only a century after Constantine's conversion. Set against the backdrop of a city that is undoubtedly Jerusalem, a golden, bejeweled cross stands above the enthroned Christ on the hill of Golgotha. This form of cross is called a *crux gemmata*: a gemmed cross. There are many instances of such glorified crosses from the

A figure at prayer. (Credit: author.)

The **IXTHUS** *symbol for Christ is still well-known today.* (Credit: author.)

early church, and they show how quickly artistic depictions of the Cross entered mainstream Christian experience after Constantine cleared the way. In the San Pudenziana mosaic, Christ sits enthroned, surrounded by his apostles; other figures symbolize the four Gospel writers: a winged ox for Luke, a winged lion for Mark, a winged man for Matthew, and an eagle for John—the four living creatures described in Revelation 4:7–8. Their presence also attests to a complex, well-advanced iconography of the faith that made amazing strides in the few short decades after Christianity became a favored religion of the state.

A dove with an olive branch. (Credit: author.)

The Good Shepherd was a favorite image for early Christians. (Credit: author.)

An anchor stands for the Cross. (Credit: author.)

To summarize, changes due primarily to the new situation for Christians following 312 CE encouraged both the development of complex cross iconography and its public display. But what accounts for Tree of Life imagery as such? There are many forms of the cross that one can find in antiquity; how do we explain the particular one with which this book is concerned?

One crucial background factor is that concepts of baptism had come to include themes of Paradise and its restoration. Neophytes were taught to see their initiation by water as entry into a New Creation, which could be expounded drawing on imagery from the first creation and Eden. Thus, for instance, the nudity called for in the moment of baptismal immersion was correlated with the original situation of Adam and Eve.[30] A very early source, *The Odes of Solomon*, "defines baptism as being taken back to paradise, the land of eternal life, where blooming and fruit-bearing trees are irrigated by rivers of gladness."[31] Later writers such as Ephrem of Edessa in the East and Augustine in the West

---

30. Jensen, *Baptismal Imagery in Early Christianity*, 180–81.
31. Ibid., 183.

echoed these themes, as did many other teachers in their own catecheti-cal programs. Persons being prepared for baptism would have absorbed a well-thought-out metaphor of the Christian life as a restoration of Paradise, from the moment of their entry into the community of the church. They would, therefore, have been predisposed toward visual imagery that made the same kind of associations. Indeed, as we will see, baptisteries came to feature artistic programs that included precisely such imagery. With such ideas of Christian life as a renewal of Eden being so widespread, any further musings about the Cross as the Tree of Life would find a natural home in Paradise imagery. In retrospect, the Life-Giving Tree in the midst of the garden of Christian life would seem to be an easy iconographical extension of ancient ideas about the meaning of baptism.

However, an additional historical circumstance must be taken into account, namely the development of rites of veneration of the Wood of

The mosaic at the Church of San Pudenziana in Rome. (Credit: author.)

the True Cross, which began to emerge in fourth-century Jerusalem.[32] In time, these rituals included conceptions of that wood as itself being a source of life and healing, for such it was experienced to be. Veneration of and devotion to this most important relic of Christ was a centerpiece of the pilgrimage experience. The experience of venerating the Life-Giving Wood of the Cross helped catalyze demand for works of art that depicted the Cross as alive and as life-giving. Pilgrims who venerated the Cross in person would naturally seek ways of interpreting and visualizing their experience. Depicting the Living Wood of the Cross in the form of a Life-Giving Tree was also a natural step for artists to take, allowing the theological meaning of such personal encounters to be expressed far and wide. Since this aspect of the story is not well known to most modern Western Christians, I will dwell on it at greater length.

Constantine is involved, once again. The recovery of and devotion to the Wood of the True Cross was due to his activity. Constantine's subsidization of Christianity included a vigorous program of archeological research in Palestine, with a goal of locating, restoring, and adorning sites connected with the earthly life of Christ. We may not realize how much effort was involved. However in the three centuries since Jesus's day, Jerusalem had shrunk to a minor outpost of the empire. The Jewish infrastructure was long gone and it had become a pagan city, renamed Aelia Capitolina. Some sites thought to be connected with Jesus were occasionally visited by tourists, but overall there was little to see, and little interest in what was available to be seen.

Constantine's energetic program quickly changed all this. In a few short years, discoveries of all sorts were made, including the reputed location of the tomb where Christ was buried and the unearthing of what was thought to be very wood of the Cross of Christ near to the

---

32. That the wood thus venerated was the actual wood of the Cross was authenticated by miracle. For the intellectual difficulties this presents, see below. It is not necessary to accept that the wood that was venerated was the real historical wood of Jesus's Cross to appreciate the impact that such veneration would have had for persons who did hold this belief.

traditional site of Golgotha.³³ Constantine subsidized the construction of a magnificent new edifice to house them all, the structure that today is called the Church of the Holy Sepulcher by Western Christians and the "Anastasis" (or "Resurrection") by Eastern Christians. Visitors to the church complex were shown not only the wood, but also the title written by Pilate, "This is Jesus, the King of the Jews" (Matt. 27:37). Both were safeguarded in a splendid silver casket, and brought out on special occasions, especially Good Friday and the festival of the Dedication of the Church of the Holy Sepulcher in mid-September. Even amid all the tangible ways the Holy Land offered pilgrims the opportunity to feel close to Christ, this wood stood out. John of Damascus, writing after the Muslim conquests, explained: "That honorable and most truly venerable tree upon which Christ offered himself as a sacrifice for us is itself to be adored, because it has been sanctified by contact with the sacred body and blood."³⁴

Coming to terms with this understanding of the True Cross will take some mental recalibration for many people. For the past thousand years, relics of the True Cross have been an occasion for mockery and fun. The little splinters of wood that were palmed off on the credulous in the Middle Ages have become a standing joke. That one could build a fleet of ships with all the reputed shards is but one example. We skeptical moderns come to a consideration of the early cult of the Cross with some long-standing prejudices. Adding to the difficulties of anyone who might wish to explore it is the simple fact that the original timbers which were used in that cult have long since disappeared. That there was a time when there were extant not mere splinters, but a sizable piece of wood, is forgotten.

A visual tradition that can help us visualize the early perspective is the iconography of the Eastern Orthodox Church. The icon of the

33. Tradition has attributed this discovery to the supervision of Constantine's mother, Helena, who was sent to Palestine to demonstrate the Imperial interest in Christian archeology. The emperor himself never visited the holy sites he patronized.
34. John of Damascus, Orth. Faith, 4:11, quoted in Vikan, *Byzantine Pilgrimage Art*, 5.

Exaltation of the Cross, used especially on that feast day in mid-September, is instructive.

The icon depicts the bishop and two deacons holding the wooden cross aloft for worshippers (including Constantine and Helena) to adore. The wood held aloft in ancient times was probably just a single beam. Nevertheless a scene such as that depicted here is probably similar to what early visitors to Jerusalem experienced. The history of Holy Cross Day and its rituals will be described more fully in chapter four. Suffice it to say for now that the origin of the feast was a liturgical event in which a sizable piece of wood, which everyone involved sincerely believed to be the wood on which Christ died, was thus elevated before the people. An equally compelling liturgy took place on Good Friday, when the actual wood of the Cross was presented to worshippers for individual veneration. A line of worshippers came single file into the presence of the Wood, which was held carefully by the bishop and two deacons. Each worshipper bowed before the Wood and kissed it before moving on.[35]

We might well ponder how we would feel had we held such a belief and been present on—for instance—Good Friday. What other tangible object could be so profoundly touching to believers as the wood that they sincerely believed to have been honored by Christ himself with his Passion? When we begin to comprehend the feelings of those early worshippers, our sympathies for them may be increased. We may still entertain modern doubts that the wood so venerated was "really" the Cross of Christ. We can have no doubts, however, about the depth and authenticity of feeling that those early worshippers experienced. Their feelings of devotion and awe must surely be respected.

It will also illuminate what is to follow to remember that early Christians also believed that the numinous power of one relic could be transferred to another physical object. Ancient pilgrims called such objects "blessings." The modern idea of bringing home souvenirs is a good comparison. What modern-day visitor to the Holy Land has not

---

35. Jensen, *The Cross: History, Art, and Controversy*, 62–63.

This icon based on Eastern Orthodox tradition is found in an Anglican setting, the altar cross at Holy Cross Monastery in West Park, New York. (Credit: Brother Randy Greve; used with permission.)

come back with one or more reminders of the special sense of presence felt there? I myself treasure a simple beeswax candle that I was given in the grotto of the Church of the Nativity in Bethlehem. The members of my tour group were all given such candles. After praying and lighting them from a nearby flame that marks the reputed place of Christ's birth, we sang "Away in a Manger" in hushed tones. We extinguished our candles and moved on, but it is impossible for me to feel that this candle is now an ordinary one. I use it each year to light the Christ candle at the beginning of Christmas Eve services and explain the origin of the candle to awestruck children. The feeling of connectedness with Christ's own birth in Bethlehem is undeniable. The candle is indeed a "blessing."

Ancient pilgrims felt just as strongly about the objects they brought home. Gary Vikan has written a very helpful account of their variety.[36]

---

36. Vikan, *Byzantine Pilgrimage Art.*

The most pertinent examples for our purposes are some small oil flasks called "ampullae." They matter to our story because they were in all probability held in direct contact with the reputed Wood of the True Cross, so as to transfer to the oil they contained the life-giving properties believed to inhere in that wood. A number of these flasks still exist in monastic treasuries in Northern Italy, carefully preserved since the sixth century when anonymous pilgrims brought them from Jerusalem. The oil they carried was valued for its medicinal and apotropaic (evil-averting) qualities. A contemporary account of how they came into contact with the Wood of the Cross reveals much about how ancient Christians regarded that wood. An anonymous pilgrim from Piacenza explained how they were created. The pilgrim first describes the liturgical veneration of the Cross and then adds: "While they are venerating the Cross . . . they offer oil to be blessed in little flasks. When the mouth of one of the little flasks touches the Wood of the Cross, the oil instantly bubbles over; and unless it is closed very quickly it all spills out."[37] The wood that the flasks touched must therefore have been regarded as having remarkable powers. In the second chapter we will consider the fascinating artwork on one of these lovely ampullae, which will give us even more insight into how the Wood of the Cross was viewed.

Given all of the above, that the imagery of the Cross came to be identified with the Tree of Life is not surprising. The site of the Crucifixion in Jerusalem had long since been identified with the location of Eden; the Wood venerated there was experienced as a source of power; literary sources had already worked out a typology of Cross and Tree; baptismal candidates understood their sharing in the death of Christ to be their entry into a restored Paradise. What could be more natural than to see continuity between the original Tree of Life and the "Tree" on which Christ wrought salvation? As we shall see, ancient artists developed precisely such depictions. The conflation of Tree and Cross was developed in a variety of media: mosaic, tapestry, carvings, and metalwork, to name

---

37. Vikan, *Byzantine Pilgrimage Art,* 11.

but a few. Working in these media, artists created a compelling suite of symbols to convey their vision. One simple image combined past, present, and future in a single vision of God's redemptive action in Christ. That ancient Christians appreciated such imagery is amply confirmed by its wide distribution. As we will see, crosses influenced by the identification with the Tree of Life are found in Scotland, Tibet, India, Rome, Armenia, Ethiopia, Northern Africa, and Egypt. It was a visual symbol of great value to the most successful evangelistic era of Christian history. The appeal of the New Creation that it depicted was a visual message that accompanied the gospel to every land.

There is one more point some readers may have wondered about: how can the imagery of a Life-Giving Cross can be reconciled to the crucifixes with which many are familiar, depicting a dead or dying Christ? The answer is that the latter images were less common in the first millennium than we might suppose. To be sure there were images of Christ crucified: the High Crosses of Ireland, for example, which date to the ninth century and possibly earlier. However on those crosses Jesus, though crucified, is very much alive. On the west face of the Cross of Muiredach at Monasterboice, the crucified Christ stands tall and extends his arms in blessing. His open hands are larger than life.

Praying before such art, one is moved to reflect not on Jesus's agony, but on the calm confidence of his victory. Art forms whose visual interest centers on the suffering and death of Christ came later. The first Western cross to exhibit this interest fully is the Gero crucifix found in the Bonn Cathedral and dated to 970 CE. Robin Jensen comments:

> The image of Christ crucified is so ubiquitous in Christian art that it seems impossible that it was not there from the first. Yet, art historians have been unable to identify an unambiguously Christian crucifix prior to the fourth or early fifth century, and only a few examples before the sixth century.[38]

---

38. Jensen, *The Cross: History, Art, and Controversy*, 74.

Louis van Tongeren puts it this way:

> [In] the image that dominates the early medieval iconography of
> the cross . . . Christ is portrayed standing on the cross as the liv-
> ing conqueror, the king who reigns from the cross. The crucifixion
> scene was only rarely depicted during this period. In the second
> millennium, by contrast, a different image prevailed: that of Christ
> hanging on the cross as a suffering, bleeding, and humiliated man,
> crowned with thorns. In the early Middle Ages, the cross was
> the tool of victory and not yet the instrument of passion it would
> become in the Middle Ages.[39]

Robin Jensen reflects at length about possible reasons for the late
appearance of both cross and crucifix in art, and the interested reader

*The High Cross of Muiredach at Monasterboice in Ireland. This beautiful cross
is particularly well preserved due to the hardness of the stone from which it is
carved.* (Credit: author.)

---

39. van Tongeren et al., "Imagining the Cross on Good Friday," 51.

The Gero crucifix in the Cathedral at Bonn is one of the earliest examples of the crucifix with a dead Christ. (Credit: Elke Wetzig, Creative Commons GNU Free Document License.)

is referred to her work.[40] Suffice it to say that a principal goal of this book is to reimagine a Christian world in which worshippers were highly aware of the rejuvenating aspects of the primary Christian symbol, and in which cross images of the dead and dying Christ had not yet come to the preeminence we assume they always must have had.

It does indeed take an act of imagination to put ourselves back into the mental world of Christians of the first millennium. Odd though it sounds to us, they did not connect the Cross only with death and suffering. We have inherited a tradition that has been oriented to the crucifix for a millennium and thus we make such connections instinctively, but in earlier times this was not so much the case. The Cross has always been a reminder of Christ's death, but believers of the first millennium also saw it as a symbol of New Creation.

---

40. Jensen, *The Cross: History, Art, and Controversy,* especially chapter four *"Crux Abscondita*: The Late-Emerging Crucifix."

Going Deeper

This book will invite readers to experience the theme of New Creation as a living one. As part of this strategy, each chapter includes exercises or questions to encourage personal appropriation of its contents. Such exercises will perhaps be easier when Scripture or art are their material, but history can come alive too. After all, early Christians are even now our colleagues in the communion of saints. That we might enter into their faith lives, I offer the following questions to be pondered and, if possible, discussed in small groups.

- How important are visual representations of the Cross to the practice of faith?
- What would it have felt like to live in the earliest centuries when crosses appeared only in veiled forms such as an anchor or a plough? Would anything essential have been missing?
- There have long been Christians who like Egeria yearn to walk where Christ did, and others like Gregory of Nyssa who say such pilgrimage is not necessary for faith. Where do you fall in that spectrum?
- Early Christians believed quite literally that the cross on which Jesus died had been recovered and could be venerated in person at the Church of the Holy Sepulcher. Using imagination, and setting aside modern skepticism for a moment, how would you feel if you did indeed find yourself in the presence of the actual wood of Jesus's Cross?
- Christians everywhere were shocked and baffled when Jerusalem and the Holy Land were taken by the armies of Islam. Why did God permit this disaster? they asked themselves. What do you make of the development? Is it possible that Christianity is healthier without possessing a Holy City and a New Temple, or was something important to our faith irretrievably lost?

2

Images of the Life-Giving Tree

The kingdom of heaven is like a mustard seed that someone took and sowed in his field; it is the smallest of all the seeds, but when it is grown it is the greatest of shrubs and becomes a tree, so that the birds of the air come and make nests in its branches.
—Matt. 13:31–32

Imagery based on the identification of Cross as Life-Giving Tree was widespread in the ancient world. But how did early Christian artists feel and think about this imagery and the works of art that conveyed it? What did those who paid for such images, or simply used them in their religious life, understand them to be expressing? How did those lively crosses affect prayer and worship and evangelism? The best way to answer such questions is to look at a number of examples, which is the purpose of this chapter. Looking at them and their geographical distribution will also help us to come to terms with their ubiquity in the Christianity of the first millennium.

An Ancient Ampulla

The design on one of the early ampullae described in chapter one will be our first example. A close look at it will help us understand the unique "blessing" these oil-bearing flasks were understood to carry. Ampullae are small round metal flasks covered by molded ceramic disks. The ceramic disks display carefully designed artistic programs. Inasmuch as different flasks can have identical artwork, it is clear that their disks come from the same mold. The disks are only about three inches across, but contain complex iconography in that small compass. Two representative ampullae which today are in the monastic treasury of Monza in Italy are among about thirty that have survived the years. That there are so many indicates they were once quite common, and the fact that the monastery at Monza preserved them (as did another monastery in Bobbio) tells us they were highly esteemed. They were mass-produced, but apparently much valued. The two flasks depicted below have the same artistic program, but they are not identical, a sign that the same

Two small metal oil flasks from the monastic treasury of Monza in Northern Italy. The legend in Greek letters could be translated either "Oil of the living wood of the holy places of Christ," or "Oil of the tree of life of the holy places of Christ." Pilgrims to Jerusalem brought these ampullae back to Italy between 550 and 600 CE. *(Credit: Foto Marburg/Art Resource, NY.)*

iconographical scheme was present in the minds of different artists. The description that follows is of the ampulla on the right.

The ampulla has two registers on its front. The upper register is centered on the Cross, above which the bust of Christ floats within a cruciform halo. Christ is not depicted as being crucified, that is, his body does not appear. (On other ampullae, Christ is shown affixed to the Cross.) The Cross is of Latin form, with a vertical shaft that is longer than the two arms. It is made of palm trunks and each arm has buds on the extremity, indicating that it is living wood, and it stands in the crevice of a stony outcropping representing the hill of Golgotha. Four small rivulets of water emerge from the outcropping, representing the four rivers of Eden—reminding us of the convention that Jerusalem and the Garden of Eden were in the same location.[41]

Several individuals are depicted with Christ. On either side are the two thieves who were crucified with him. The good thief turns toward Christ while the scoffing thief turns away. Unlike Christ, the bodies of the two thieves are shown in full: they are depicted in the moment of crucifixion, their open hands nailed to their respective crosses. To the extreme left of the scene, Mary, the mother of Jesus, looks on in a posture of grief. To the extreme right, John the beloved disciple also is present, but with right arm raised in the manner of an orator, and a closed book in his left hand. Kneeling at the foot of the Cross in gestures of adoration are two persons clad in contemporary Byzantine attire. Also in the scene are representations of sun and moon on either side of the bust of Christ. They turn away in cosmic sorrow.

The lower register of the ampulla depicts resurrection. It is centered on the structure that houses the tomb of Christ in the Church of the Holy Sepulcher, called the "edicule." This appears in somewhat schematic form with a cross at its top. To the left of the edicule we see the two Marys approaching. One carries a flask of ointment; the other carries a

---

41. This description is indebted to the work of Andre Grabar. See Grabar, *Ampoules de terre Sainte.*

censer such as would be used liturgically. To the right, the angel awaits the two Marys with raised arm. Immediately above the edicule are the words of angelic greeting (in Greek), "The Lord is risen."

The upper register at first glance appears to be a depiction of the historic crucifixion of Christ as recounted in the Gospels. Thus we see the central Cross flanked by the two crucified thieves, Mary on the left and John on the right, and the symbols of sun and moon. However, further inspection quickly makes it evident that the depiction has aspects that were *not* part of the historical crucifixion. An artist's representation of the central scene provides a clearer picture.

The two pilgrims who venerate the Cross are visitors to Jerusalem in Byzantine times, more than five centuries after the Crucifixion, and dressed in clothing of the day. Christ gazes purposefully into eternity, encircled in a halo, and is not fixed to the Cross, but floats above it.

An artist's close-up of the upper register of the Monza ampulla, showing its central scene. Note the living palm-tree buds of the Cross and the four rivers of Paradise coming forth from the rock of Calvary. (Credit: Aidan O'Flynn.)

The wood of the Cross is made of palm trunks and appears to be alive, thus representing the Tree of Life, reinforcing the inference that the Crucifixion took place in the same location as the original Garden of Eden. From the rock of Calvary flow the four rivers of Paradise, recalling the connection with Eden, but also alluding to the river of the water of life as described in Revelation 21–22, where this river is adjacent to the Tree of Life in the heavenly Jerusalem. Thus in addition to the historical setting of Christ's death, ca. 30 CE, on the metaphorical level we find both the Garden of Eden and the heavenly Jerusalem, the beginning and the end. The two contemporary worshippers anchor it all in contemporary times—contemporary for the pilgrims, that is—550–600 CE. Multiple meanings are therefore presented as occurring in one simultaneous vista.

The theological message of this multivalent imagery depends heavily on the identification of the Cross as the Tree of Life—a tree described both in Genesis and in the Revelation to John. The iconography of the ampulla thus proclaims that through the Cross Christ has reopened paradise and conferred on humanity the immortality so long denied us. In the present, Christ pours upon us healing streams of spiritual blessing. Christ's presence in the center of the restored creation therefore fully merits the rapt devotion of contemporary worshippers, evoking Revelation 22:3–4: "His servants will worship him; they will see his face."

The historical and theological aspects together recall the inner meaning of the experiences of pilgrims at the holy site of Golgotha. The pilgrims' devotional experiences before the Wood of the True Cross, described in both chapters one and four, inserted them into this complex series of stories, beginning in creation and ending at the consummation of all things. The Crucifixion of Christ—the actual historical event—was at the center of the series, and the liturgies of the Holy Sepulcher made the entire saving narrative a tangible experience of grace. The oil and the ampulla concretized all this grace, making it both portable and durable.

The final piece of the puzzle, however, is the text found on the ampulla. Surrounding both scenes in a double-bordered circle is a legend written in Greek, which could be translated as "oil of the living wood of the holy places of Christ." However, it could just as well be understood as the "oil of the tree of life of the holy places of Christ." The Greek words found on the legend are the same words that in Revelation 22 are translated as the "Tree of Life" and, for that matter, the same words found in the Greek version of the Old Testament, the Septuagint, in Genesis 2, where the Tree of Life is first mentioned.

So the legend on the ampulla also carries multiple levels of meaning. It affirms that the wood of the holy places of Christ is living wood, that it gives life, and that it is in fact the Tree of Life. Christ's Cross has come to be experienced as a continuing source of life and power, a sacrament of resurrection. The oil of the ampulla was therefore understood to be "Tree of Life Oil." No wonder the little flasks were treasured as blessings, and preserved as tokens for the faithful.

A Byzantine-Era Floor Mosaic

The ancient Byzantine church complex at Oued Ramel in Tunisia was described by Paul Gauckler in 1913.[42] He found it largely in ruins, but excavation of the baptistery revealed the font with an adjacent floor mosaic still largely intact. Because they were at ground level, the mosaic and font were less susceptible to damage than the buildings that had formerly housed them. They were covered over by soil and their remarkable imagery was protected through the centuries. Gauckler's drawings are the basis of this description that follows.[43]

The baptismal font itself was in the shape of a cross. The four arms of the cross opened from ground level down into the pool. People being baptized would walk down into the water, using steps set into the cross arms, to a maximum depth of 1.1 meters at the center. Four columns formerly supported a dome over the font; in 1913 only one of the four was still visible. We must therefore imagine a rectangular building containing

---

42. Gauckler, *Basiliques Chrétiennes de Tunisie (1892–1904)*, pl. XVIII.
43. I wish to thank the Reverend Joan Fleming for assistance in translating Gauckler's text.

An artist's rendering of Gauckler's sketch of the floor mosaic of the Byzantine-era church in Oued Ramel, Tunisia. The cross shape in the center is the font that persons being baptized entered down three steps. (Credit: Aidan O'Flynn.)

a cross-shaped pool covered by an interior dome-like structure. The room as a whole was about four meters long, and the now-vanished walls probably had painted scenes as well, depicting episodes from Scripture. The baptistery was oriented to the cardinal directions.

Around the cross-shaped font was the mosaic floor with its profusion of iconographic features. Entering from the west end, one would first encounter the four rivers of Paradise issuing from a large scalloped shell at the base of the cross-shaped font. On either side of the rivers were two deer drinking from the four rivers: to the right a buck with antlers, and to the left (with only the head still intact in 1913) the matching doe. From the sides of the cross-font four palm trees grew, laden with fruit. At the far end of the cross, reversed in orientation from the water-drinking deer, two peacocks framed a central vase, which also had a scalloped appearance. The peacocks, in turn, were framed by flowers. At the center of the cross, at its maximum depth, a dove in flight completed the artistic program.

How would such a font and such imagery actually have been used? We do not have extensive literary accounts of baptism for this period in North Africa as we do for other parts of the ancient Christian world. However, it is possible to tease out hints from earlier writers such as

Augustine and Cyprian that indicate the pattern of Christian initiation there was broadly similar to what was practiced elsewhere. Paul Gauckler concluded, on the basis of similarities with other known sites, that the Oued Ramel complex was from the Byzantine period—at a time when the region was ruled from Constantinople. It seems reasonable to assume, therefore, that what we know from other Byzantine and late antique sources would apply to the Oued Ramel baptistery as well. The pattern of initiatory rites had three basic stages: admission to the catechumenate; enrollment as a candidate for baptism; and the rites of initiation. According to liturgical scholar Edward Yarnold, "Many of these individual ceremonies remained recognizably the same everywhere."[44]

At their admission to the catechumenate (that is, to the status of "hearers" of the liturgy but not yet permitted to receive communion) the sign of the cross was traced on the foreheads of new believers. Salt was placed on their tongues signifying healing, preservation, and wisdom. They also received prayer with the laying on of hands, and an exorcism. This took place as much as three years prior to the actual baptism.

Enrollment as a candidate typically took place forty days prior to baptism, with Lent providing the normal period of final preparation. This period would include intense study and further repeated exorcisms, in addition to keeping the fast. The final rites of initiation usually took place during the night between Holy Saturday and Easter morn, presided over by the bishop in person. The ceremonies began in an outside room of the baptistery where the candidates stripped to receive a pre-baptismal anointing of the whole body, which was followed by a formal renunciation of the devil and a statement of loyalty to Christ. The baptismal waters were then exorcised and blessed by the power of the Holy Spirit. The candidates stepped down into the waters, where they were immersed three times.

Since the font at Oued Ramel was not deep enough for easy total immersion, it is likely that the bishop poured water three times from

44. Jones, Wainwright, Yarnold, and Bradshaw, *The Study of Liturgy*, 95.

above, while the candidate confessed faith in the three Persons of the Trinity. The candidate's head was then anointed with oil of chrism. When the candidate came up from the water, the bishop and clergy washed their feet, and dressed them in a white robe, which they wore for the whole of Easter week. In many cases the newly baptized person was given a lighted candle. Their initiation was completed when they entered the nearby church to participate in the action of Holy Eucharist for the first time.[45]

The artistic layout of the Oued Ramel floor mosaic would have helped explain the meaning of baptism, beginning with the cross-shaped font which is part of the picture in its own right. The candidate's immersion in its waters could easily be interpreted as a conforming to the Cross of Christ.[46] This reminds us of Paul's words to the Romans, "Do you not know that all of us who have been baptized into Christ were baptized into his death?" (Rom. 6:3).

At the base of the cross the four streams of Paradise descend from a scalloped shell, itself a water motif that is a common symbol for baptism. Thus, as in the Monza ampulla, the Cross is depicted as standing in Paradise. As was mentioned in the previous chapter, early teachers expounded baptism as entry into Paradise, so it is easy to imagine an ancient cleric drawing upon the artistic scheme of the Oued Ramel baptistery to make this point while preparing candidates.

The rivers flowing out from Golgotha at the center of the garden provide refreshment for two deer. The deer easily put us in mind of Psalm 42, which was sung at the beginning of the ancient baptismal rite:[47]

> As a deer longs for flowing streams, so my soul longs for you, O God. My soul thirsts for God, for the living God. (Ps. 42:1–2)

---

45. Ibid., 95–110.
46. For other early artifacts with similar symbolic schemes, see Noga-Banai and Safran, "A Late Antique Silver Reliquary in Toronto," 16–19.
47. Jensen, *Baptismal Imagery in Early Christianity*, 212.

The deer's drinking symbolizes the spiritual thirst that has brought the candidates to Christ. Baptism—conformity to Christ—will quench the dryness of their souls; for them it is the spring of water welling up to eternal life. The fruitful palm trees on either side of the cross-font are the trees of Paradise amid which the Cross, the Tree of Life, is to be found. The same scriptural resonances that we have already seen on the Monza ampulla are present here also. The palms remind us of the leaves of the Tree of Life, for the healing of the nations, and the ripe fruits bespeak divine abundance.

At the center of the font is its lowest point, where the candidate would have stood for the actual baptism. The bird in flight at the center represents the dove of the Holy Spirit who descended upon Christ at his baptism. It would remind the candidate of God's words to Jesus at that moment, "You are my Son, the Beloved; with you I am well pleased" (Mark 1:11). No more touching reminder of an intimacy restored could be imagined: the alienation of humanity from God symbolized by the story of the loss of Eden is overcome by the power of the Spirit.

Finally, at the east end of the font are the twin peacocks and an urn amid the flowers. The peacocks represent immortal life: in ancient times it was thought that the flesh of peacocks did not decay, hence the symbolism of eternity. The urn in the shape of a scallop shell is another reminder of water, and the flowers represent the happy fields of Paradise.

The floor mosaic as a whole therefore is an invitation to ponder progress in the spiritual life. Beginning with thirsty souls, the candidates ascend the rivers of Paradise to their source, which is the Cross of Christ. The candidates step over the shell (which heightens the water imagery) and then climb down into the water. Professing faith in the Father, the Son, and the Holy Spirit, they are immersed or drenched from above three times. Holy intimacy with God is pronounced, and spiritual connection is restored, as symbolized by the flight of the heavenly dove. Then the candidates ascend out of the font, moving amid the trees of Paradise and into its flowery meadows. Friendly beings, peacocks and deer, share the divinely appointed luster of a New Creation. It is an overwhelming array of blessings that shower upon the newly born Christian, as he or she steps out into a New Creation.

St. John Lateran Apse Mosaic

The baptistery floor of an obscure North African church gives one example of Paradise imagery from the ancient church. But is this symbolism also found in more prominent venues? Its presence in a mosaic in the apse[48] of St. John Lateran Church in Rome allows an emphatic "yes" for an answer. This remarkable basilica was donated by Constantine I and dedicated by Pope Sylvester I in 324 CE to serve as the cathedra of the bishop of Rome. It would be hard to find a venue more prominent than that! The apse mosaic features themes that should already be familiar from these pages. Admittedly, the mosaic as it appears today is relatively modern. However, Robin Jensen notes:

> Although the current apse mosaic was installed at the end of the nineteenth century when the church was extended, its composition may be based on the prior mosaic, created by Jacopo Torriti along with the Franciscan Jacopo Camerino in the late thirteenth century, which in turn may have been inspired by an underlying, late antique model.[49]

The cross itself is a gem-encrusted *crux gemmata* (gemmed cross), but its shape is reminiscent of the living palm tree of the Monza ampulla. From above, the dove of the Holy Spirit emits a stream of water from its beak that cascades down both sides of the cross into a pool at its base. From the pool, the water descends through the four rivers of Paradise—individually labelled as Gihon, Pishon, Tigris, and Euphrates—to emerge into the River Jordan at the bottom. Two antlered deer drink from the rivers, accompanied in this case by six lambs, all set among many flowers

---

48. An apse is an architectural feature of churches, meaning a recessed area behind the altar, beneath a semicircular dome. Apses are usually decorated with mosaics or other artwork.
49. Jensen, *The Cross: History, Art, and Controversy,* 148–49.

The apse mosaic of St. John Lateran basilica in Rome. (Credit: Robin Jensen; used by permission.)

and green grass. Tiny human figures disport themselves in the Jordan, engaged in such activities as fishing, swimming, and even windsurfing. The humans are joined in the Jordan by swans and sea creatures. Below the cross, and between the four rivers, "a phoenix perches in a palm that rises from the jeweled and golden city walls of the Heavenly Jerusalem; a cherub guards its gates with a drawn sword."[50] One last touch completes the watery associations: an oval medallion in the center of the cross depicts Jesus's baptism by John.

What is the overall effect on the viewer? Perhaps it is similar to the feelings of the permanent witnesses to the scene—saints including Mary,

---

50. Ibid., 149.

the mother of Jesus, and the Beloved Disciple. They stand near and render homage at the dynamic vista before them, each with one hand raised. Indeed everything about the vista is dynamic: living water—gifted by the Spirit and touched by the Life-Giving Tree—irradiates creation with freshness and vitality. The almost comic activities of the tiny humans playing in the River Jordan are quite daring. This Paradise looks fun. The saints looking on seem almost out of place with their traditional pious poses. Still, as they know well, the Spirit moves where and as the Spirit wills, and in this case it seems evident that the New Creation, like Leviathan himself, is something God has made for the sport of it.

A Coptic Sanctuary Curtain

It is unusual for textiles to survive from antiquity into modern times, especially in regions with moist climates. However, cloth objects from desert climates such as Egypt have a better chance of survival. A woven cloth panel dated to the fifth or six centuries, now in the collections of the Minneapolis Institute of Arts (MIA), is an exceptional example. Not only is the fabric itself in remarkably good condition, but its striking cross iconography makes it of particular interest to this study. It witnesses to many familiar themes from antiquity combined in a uniquely intriguing composition. The description that follows depends heavily on the work of MIA former curator Lotus Stack.[51]

Although little is known about its provenance, the available evidence suggests that the cloth panel was used liturgically as a sanctuary curtain. In the Coptic eucharistic liturgy, these curtains are drawn across the sanctuary at certain points and then drawn back. The Minneapolis panel shows signs of wear that would be consistent with such repeated folding and unfolding. Furthermore, sanctuary curtains frequently have a Cross design, as does the Minneapolis panel. It may also have been used

---

51. Stack, *A Christian Cross: A Woven Representation at the Minneapolis Institute of Arts.* I would also like to thank Dr. Jan-Lodewijk Grootaers and the museum staff for arranging a special viewing of the curtain. It is a truly beautiful object and spending time in its presence was a great privilege.

Unknown Artist, Coptic, 5th–6th century curtain, linen, wool; tapestry weave, 54 1/2 x 27 1/2 in. Minneapolis Institute of Art, The Centennial Fund: Aimee Mott Butler Charitable Trust, Mr. and Mrs. John F. Donovan, Estate of Margaret B. Hawks, Eleanor Weld Reid 83.126. (Credit: Minneapolis Institute of Art; used by permission.)

subsequently as a burial pall. If so, the conditions of interment would have protected it from exposure to moisture and weathering, and would account for its good state of preservation.

The panel is rectangular, expertly woven from linen and wool. The background is undecorated. The areas that contain designs are a tapestry structure on a base created of combined units of the warp threads. The principal design on the panel is a cross of the Latin form, whose vertical axis is longer than the arms. The four terminals are flared at their ends. At the bottom of the vertical beam, an extension fits into a separate base in tongue and groove design. A circular wreath is depicted behind the intersection of the cross arms, set around an inner ring made of four rounded quadrants. Along the perimeter, rosettes and leaf forms frame the cross on either side. The cross itself is a light orange color, outlined with a narrow band of tan and brown. Ten rectangular jewels formed of green and orange triangles decorate the vertical beam, intersecting a horizontal row of jewels of identical design, sixteen in all. Each jewel is surrounded by twelve small white pearls. The green base is also decorated with pearls, nine in number. The wreath contains twelve pieces of fruit inside a perimeter of small green leaves. Each quadrant within the wreath is decorated with a small cross, two red and two white. The wreath is depicted as though hanging behind the cross, which is seen in its entirety.

The Minneapolis cloth panel in all probability dates from the Coptic era in Egyptian history—the period from the fourth to early seventh centuries during which Egypt was an integral part of the Byzantine world and Christianity was the dominant religion. Egyptian bishops, such as Athanasius and Cyril of Alexandria, were leading figures in the theological controversies of the time, while monastic exemplars, such as Antony of Egypt, created spiritual praxes that are influential to our own day. Following the Council of Chalcedon in 451 CE, Coptic Christians continued to follow the teachings of Cyril in opposition to the official position of the Byzantine state. The persecution of the Coptic Church that ensued created an enduring bitterness, but the enthusiastic practice of Christianity in Egypt continued unabated. Major metropolitan areas and poorer rural areas alike were populated with parish churches, and the numerous remote monastic settings were famous throughout the Christian world.

A rich liturgical life was and is expressed in Coptic worship. Jewel-encrusted crosses would have been part of that liturgy in ancient times, especially in wealthier settings. The concept of a *crux gemmata* was well known throughout the late antique world, as shown in surviving mosaics in Rome and Ravenna. However, the weaver of the Minneapolis panel probably meant to depict an actual liturgical object that would have been familiar to worshippers in the locality. The original object could have been a metal cross with jewels, or it could also have been a less expensive wooden copy decorated with colored glass. An example of this humbler type is in the Cairo Museum. The fact that it is depicted resting in a base indicates an original that could have been lifted in and out, presumably to be carried in processions and then returned to a stationary place where it would be visible. The fruited wreath may have been part of a special liturgical observance, such as the Exaltation of the Cross.

The sanctuary curtain itself is a liturgical feature that is unfamiliar to most Western Christians. In the Coptic liturgy, it serves to screen off the clergy in the sanctuary at certain times, such as when the priests receive communion. At the beginning of the liturgy, the curtain is in its retracted mode, allowing the liturgical action to be witnessed by all. Then, at the appropriate times it is pulled across, hanging from a suspended line. It screens the proceedings for an interval, and then is retracted once again. Every celebration of the Eucharist therefore includes periods in which the curtain with its designs is the primary visual focus for the congregation. Music and chanting continue, but there is no action to observe when the curtain is on display. Symbols like the Cross provide an object for meditation for the people during their time of waiting.

A final use for the curtain could have been as a pall at the time of death of an important ecclesiastical individual, a practice mentioned in a letter to the Bishop of Jerusalem in the fourth century.[52] A beautiful but somewhat worn fabric, such as the Minneapolis panel, would indeed have made a suitable burial pall. A circumstantial clue in this regard is the fact that the panel has survived at all: had it been used in a dry above-ground tomb it would have been less prone to deteriorate over time. In this case, after many years of service as the devotional focus of the people, our panel would have given honor to the grave of one of their leaders.

The Cross is the central image of the panel. This is noteworthy in its own right. In no other known late antique or early medieval textile panel does a cross so dominate the design; when the cross appeared

---

52. Ibid., 4.

in woven form at this time it was almost always relatively small and subordinate to the main design.[53]

Another notable feature of the cross is that it is of the Latin form. Again, this is unusual in that most textiles surviving from this period employ the Greek (equal-armed) cross.[54] To modern Western eyes, long accustomed to Latin crosses as a dominant feature of a design, the panel probably seems more common than it would have to its ancient viewers. The most likely explanation for the Latin shape in this case is that it was intended as the depiction of a processional cross; the long vertical beam of such an object would facilitate its being carried.

The other noteworthy design element is the circular wreath affixed to the back of the cross. A wreath in antiquity would have been connected with notions of victory, hearkening back as far as the laurel wreaths awarded in Olympic games. Numerous examples of wreaths paired with emblems of Christ are known from the period. Their clear intent is to celebrate Christ's victory over sin, death, and the devil.

The relationship between these two design elements is worth pondering for two reasons. First, the wreath on the Minneapolis panel is smaller in scale and thus subordinate to the cross. Once again, this is distinctive: in the other examples known to us "the wreath-circle form and the image representing Christ most often are of equal size and design weight."[55] Second, on our panel the cross and the wreath are conjoined into a single visual statement. In the other examples known to us, the emblem of Christ is primary and the wreath, while of equal size, plays an independent supporting role. That the wreath and the cross function together may also indicate that the ancient weaver was copying an actual processional cross with an actual wreath attached.

Both the cross and the wreath have iconographically important decorations. The jewels on the cross have already been mentioned. The light

---

53. Ibid., 1.
54. Ibid., 3.
55. Ibid., 2.

orange color of the cross is intended to represent gold. The combination recalls the mosaics at San Pudenziana and in Ravenna, which in turn echo the jeweled cross that at a later time was said possibly to have been placed at Golgotha itself. *Crux gemmata* symbolism is triumphal, harkening back to the shimmering gold of Constantine's labarum, and perhaps also forward to the shimmering "sign of the Son of Man" expected in the skies of the last days. The pearls surrounding each of the jewels augment their magnificence.

The wreath bears twelve pieces of fruit, recalling the fruit-bearing Tree of Life described in the Revelation to John with its twelve kinds of fruit. The leaves along its perimeter also remind us of that Tree, whose leaves are for the healing of the nations. The overall effect is of verdant life-giving energy. Within the wreath, the four small equal-armed crosses reiterate the importance of this primary symbol.

Numerology is also undoubtedly important to the design. The four small crosses recall the four Gospels and their four authors. Twelve pieces of fruit, and twelve pearls round each of the jewels, remind us of the twelve apostles. The sixteen jewels that are present can symbolize the number of apostles and evangelists added together. Finally, the green base is itself decorated with nine pearls, three times the three of the Christian Trinity.

Taken as a whole, the curtain's design scheme would have amply rewarded meditation, especially during the times in the liturgy when it was drawn wide for the congregation to view. The panel has a rich set of associations worthy of repeated periods of reflection. The cross itself represents Christ victorious. The wreath symbolizes victory and renewal of life. The jewels, pearls, and gold symbolize the splendor of the heavenly Jerusalem as well as the Coptic liturgy. The number symbolism invites reflection on the ongoing work of the Church in her apostles and evangelists. The stepped base, finally, represents the stony outcropping of Golgotha, with its carved steps, and is a humbling reminder of the actual human drama of Golgotha, where Christ made his life-giving offering for salvation. As a commentary on the eucharistic liturgy in which it was being viewed, it offered reassurance that Christ's victory continues in the lives of his followers, and a vision of the Cross as life-giving.

Vine-Scroll, Ruthwell Cross

The justly celebrated Ruthwell Cross now stands in the interior of the Church of Scotland (Presbyterian) parish in the village of Ruthwell, not too far from Glasgow. Its history into modern times is worthy of a page-turning novel. Carved and set up in a monastic compound in the eighth century, it fell afoul of iconoclastic tendencies in the Reformation and was buried by a sympathetic minister to preserve it for posterity. The Rev. Gavin Young deserves a place in the pantheon of heroes of Christian art for creatively defying a direct order from his superiors to destroy what they called an "idolatrous monument." Its disassembled pieces were used as pews for a century and more, until the Rev. Henry Duncan reassembled them in the manse garden in 1802. A photograph taken in the nineteenth century shows the scale and general form of the cross, although it should be noted that many aspects of the reconstruction would not pass critical muster today. In particular, the crossbeam at the top is not original, and the sun symbol is a nineteenth-century idea of what might have been found there. Nevertheless, the reconstruction in Duncan's photograph does a better job of conveying the effect of the whole than does the current arrangement, in which only part of the cross is visible within the sanctuary of the Ruthwell parish church. Bearing in mind also that, when first erected, the cross probably was painted brightly, it must have been an impressive sight indeed—a remarkable adjunct to the spiritual life of the monastic community that is presumed to have been its original home.

The Ruthwell Cross is somewhat earlier and of a different form than the well-known High Crosses of Ireland. The Irish Crosses have a Latin form—the shaft is longer than the cross arms—and also they typically feature a carved ring round the crossing. The Ruthwell Cross, by contrast, is of a style more common in Scotland and indeed found frequently across Europe in early times.[56] In this style, an equal-armed cross is set atop a central shaft, which is not itself part of the cross, but rather supports it. On the Ruthwell Cross the long supporting shaft provides space for the various carved scenes and their accompanying legends.

Beginning in the late eighteenth century, a succession of antiquarians and curious travelers slowly spread the fame of the Ruthwell Cross, and in particular the puzzle of certain runes inscribed on two of its sides. The eventual translation of these runes constitutes a great triumph of Anglo-Saxon scholarship.[57] Dramatic and intriguing though this story is, it exceeds the scope of the present volume. The same is true of what

Ruthwell Cross as erected by Rev. Henry Duncan in the garden of the manse, ca. 1823–1887, north side. (Credit: Dinwiddie, *The Ruthwell Cross and Its Story* (1927), fig. facing p. 107)

---

56. Kelly, "The Relationships of the Crosses of Argyll: the Evidence of Form," 219–29.
57. Cassidy, "The Later Life of the Ruthwell Cross," in *The Ruthwell Cross*, 3–4.

is admittedly the most interesting aspect of the cross: its many carved scenes and Latin inscriptions, and their iconographic interpretation.

Remarkable as the carved Scripture scenes and the runes are, our interest is in another feature of the Cross—the beautiful vine-scrolls carved on the two narrower sides. Vine-scrolls not unlike those of Ruthwell's are a frequent attribute of Anglo-Saxon carved crosses.[58] Such scrolls display sinuous grapevines gracefully enfolding the carved surfaces. If they include animal life, as Ruthwell's does, they are called "inhabited vine-scrolls." It is immediately apparent that the birds and monkeys shown feeding upon the refulgent bunches of grapes are creatures not native to Scotland. This is a clue that the antecedents of such designs derive from elsewhere. Ernst Kitzinger argued that the most likely models for such designs are certain Coptic carvings from the Byzantine era in Egypt—the same provenance as the sanctuary curtain described above.[59] In any event the motif of vibrantly ascending vines establishes them as examples of the living or life-giving tree theme we have noted elsewhere. They are intended to evoke Paradise.[60]

Yet, fascinatingly, these exuberant life-filled scenes are paired with the aforementioned carved runes, which we will now examine. The great triumph of Anglo-Saxon scholarship was to recognize the close connection of the runes with the well-known poem, *The Dream of the Rood*.[61] In this early poem, the story of the Crucifixion is told from the perspective of the Cross itself, who speaks in the first person. The Ruthwell Cross runes are much less extensive than the poem as a whole, and are not identical to it. Nevertheless, they are clearly a version of the same text. A reconstruction and translation of the verses found on the Ruthwell Cross is as follows:

58. Kitzinger, "Anglo-Saxon Vine-Scroll Ornament," 61–71.
59. Ibid.
60. Ó Carragáin, *Ritual and the Rood*, 285–92.
61. Barbara Raw argues that the same complex of meanings found in the ampullae discussed above is also found in the poem. See "The Dream of the Rood and Its Connections with Early Christian Art," 244.

God almighty stripped Himself. When He wished to ascend on the gallows, brave before all men, I dared not bow down, but had to stand fast.

I raised up a powerful King. I dared not tilt the Lord of Heaven. Men mocked us both together. I was drenched with blood issued from the Man's side after He sent forth his spirit.

Christ was on the Cross. But hastening nobles came together there from afar. I beheld it all. Sorely was I with sorrows afflicted. I bent to the men, to their hands.

Ruthwell Cross, side view showing the "inhabited vine-scroll" motif, framed by runes related to the early poem The Dream of the Rood. (Credit: author.)

Wounded with arrows they laid Him down weary in limb.
They stood for Him at the head of His corpse. They beheld there
Heaven's Lord. And He rested Himself there for a time.[62]

It would be difficult to conceive a more dramatic contrast in tone
between word and image. The vine-scrolls ascend joyfully from earth
toward heaven. The runes descend, literally, being read from above
downward, through heartfelt despair to death. Nonetheless the upward
and downward motions belong together: they form a unity. It was the
poignant dying of Jesus that won for us the New Creation, a reopened
Paradise of eucharistic sharing represented by the symbol of the True
Vine. To read the poem to its end is to have the eye drawn to the base of
the cross, from which springs upward the rejuvenating pulse of the life-
giving vine. To look to the top of the vine is to begin to reread the poem,
and to take to heart once more the unfathomable sacrifice of Jesus. The
two aspects of word and image are synergistically intertwined, and bring
alive for us the dual meaning of life from death: the essence of the mystery of Christ. Catherine Karkov explains how the viewer becomes kin-
esthetically involved in the experience of the Cross:

> The arrangement of runic inscriptions . . . necessitates the reader
> making the sign of the cross with his or her own eyes. Of equal
> significance is the fact that in reading we are forced to move our
> eyes both along and across the vine-scroll so that text and ornament
> merge. . . . The viewer becomes one with the animals nibbling at
> the bunches of grapes, and one with the cross raising aloft Christ's
> bleeding body and then lowering it to the hands of men.[63]

Jennifer O'Reilly draws all the aspects together:

> In a single unifying image the sculptural decoration of the narrow
> sides reveals Christ to be the Tree of Life, that is, the axis at the cen-
> tre of the world joining heaven and earth providing spiritual food

---

62. Howlett, "Inscriptions and Design of the Ruthwell Cross," 88.
63. Karkov, *The Art of Anglo-Saxon England*, 1:142.

and healing for all. The Tree rises the height of the towering shaft on both sides and is shown in the form of a rooted vine-scroll filled with diverse creatures feeding on its fruit. It regenerates a Mediterranean image of the incorporation of all the faithful members of the church into the sacramental and glorified body of Christ.[64]

Vine-Scrolls Compared: Anglo-Saxon and Coptic

In 1934 art historian Ernst Kitzinger raised the question of prototypes for the many instances of vine-scroll found on Anglo-Saxon crosses. After considering various alternatives, he concluded that the closest comparisons were with certain Coptic carvings of the Byzantine era.[65] While this trail of influence remains conjectural, the images from his article published in 1936 are certainly suggestive. Two works of art which he discussed are shown nearby. The elegant swirls of the Coptic artwork's vine, and even the attitude of the birds as they nibble on grapes, appear quite similar to the artwork from Scotland.

The possibility of such a connection deserves comment. Although direct lines of causality are often impossible to prove, it is hard to avoid the impression that a great many such lines did in fact exist in early times. Many have noted commonalities between, for instance, styles of monasticism in Ireland and in Egypt, or styles of book making in Africa and by Anglo-Saxon scribes. Michelle P. Brown [66] catalogues a plethora of such examples, and it was an article proposing common features between the Irish High Crosses and the Armenian khachkars that prompted my own quest.[67] One famous example of such influence from afar is Adomnán's treatise on the Holy Land called the *Loci Sancti*. Written on the tiny island of Iona off the west coast of Scotland, it purported to be based on the first-person information given by a wandering Frankish Bishop named Arculf. Coming home from the Holy Land, Adomnán said,

---

64. Quoted in Ó Carragáin, *Ritual and the Rood,* 286.
65. Kitzinger, "Anglo-Saxon Vine-Scroll Ornament."
66. Brown, "The Eastwardness of Things."
67. Richardson, "Observations on Christian Art in Early Ireland, Georgia and Armenia."

Arculf was blown off course and ended up on Iona, where he gave his information to an eager audience. Although the veracity of this account has been questioned, the mere fact that it seemed plausible (Adomnán's work enjoyed wide popularity in the Middle Ages) tells us much about the ways information could have and did flow in the first millennium. People got around and shared ideas and, although we can hardly ever know the particulars, the overall impression is that this must have been so. Indeed it would be surprising if it were not. Certainly the widespread distribution of Living Tree imagery would seem to depend on frequent sharing of ideas across many miles.

On this same theme, the Coptic sanctuary curtain described earlier has been proposed as a possible forerunner

An Anglo-Saxon vine-scroll from Jedburgh Abbey in Scotland (left) is compared to a carving from Egypt (above). Jedburgh photo by Alice Blackwell; used by permission. Fragment from a two-sided sanctuary screen. Made in Egypt, Bawit. Coptic, 5th–6th century. Limestone, H. 12 ¼ in. W. 13 3/16 in. D. 3 ¾ in. Rogers Fund, 1910 (10.175.18) The Metropolitan Museum of Art, NY, U.S.A. (Credit: Art Resource, NY)

of the Irish High Crosses. Prior to the late ninth century, there were many carved crosses in the British Isles, but the idea of carving them with a conspicuous ring was a novelty. Scholars were not at all in agreement about how they came to be.[68] After the Coptic curtain appeared at the Minneapolis Institute of the Arts in 1984, art historian Walter Horn noticed the striking resemblance of form between the High Crosses and the curtain. It was the first known cross that predates the High Crosses to have exactly the same form as they do, and so a line of influence is not impossible.[69]

Whether or not the Anglo-Saxon and Irish artists who created vine-scrolls and ringed crosses were dependent on antecedents from Egypt is impossible to know. Suffice it to say that artists from both ends of the Mediterranean created motifs that speak the same visual language and made the same kinds of appeal to the heart.

A Byzantine-Era Leaved Cross

In 1950 D. Talbot Rice drew attention to the widespread appearance of what he called the "leaved cross" motif in eastern Christian art.[70] A sketch based on one of the earliest examples in his article appears on page 61. It is a bas-relief in stone from Asia Minor, and dated to the sixth century, approximately the same time period as the ampulla, the sanctuary curtain, and the Oued Ramel baptistery considered earlier. The cross has budding features at the end of each of its four tips and a graceful flowering plant growing out of the base. The stems reach upward and three flowers stretch toward the crossbeam, almost touching them. The impression is of a cross that has sprouted into life. Talbot Rice found

---

68. A theory I heard from a Dublin tour bus guide is not likely, however: that ringed crosses were a sun motif created to appeal to pagans. Ireland had been a Christian nation for nearly four centuries before the first High Crosses were carved! Sun-worshipping pagans were not the target audience, but fearful monastic communities seeking divine protection against marauding Vikings.
69. Horn, "On the Origin of the Celtic Cross," 88–89.
70. Rice, "The Leaved Cross," 72–81.

many exemplars of the motif throughout the Eastern Christian world, and also some from the Greek- and Latin-speaking regions. He was able to show commonalities with art from Persia as well, demonstrating that the motif had wide resonance in antiquity. In any event, his conclusion was clear, that the aim of this art was to depict the Cross as the Tree of Life, and that this style was exceptionally widespread across many geographical regions.

As will become evident below, modern Christian communities descended from those who created the ancient leaved crosses have remained faithful to the motif. Oriental Orthodox churches of India, Armenia, and Ethiopia employ it to this day, as do the so-called Nestorians, who are the living representatives of what is known as the Church of the East. Since these churches are at best poorly known to Christians of the Western traditions, some basic information should be provided.

Most Western Christians are aware that there are Eastern Orthodox believers from lands such as Greece and Russia. The icons created by these churches have become popular among mainline Western Christians in recent decades. What is less appreciated is that there are other Christians even farther east who are not in communion with the

An artist's recreation of a sixth-century "leaved cross" on a bas-relief stone carving from Asia Minor. (Credit: Aidan O'Flynn)

Eastern Orthodox and who have their own distinct histories. To sort out who is who requires one to spend time with the Christological controversies of the fifth century, for it was at that epoch that fault lines that still exist today first emerged.[71]

The Nestorian Church of the East is descended from those who were on the losing side at the Council of Ephesus in 433 CE. Feeling unwelcome in the Roman Empire, they sought refuge elsewhere and soon created a vibrant church centered on Persia, and reached as far as Tibet and China. The patriarch Timothy mentioned in chapter one was of this group.

A second fault line occurred after the Council of Chalcedon in 451 CE. Although the formula of Christ as one person in two natures became the touchstone of orthodoxy in Latin- and Greek-speaking churches, elsewhere many Christians refused to accept the Council or its results. The Churches of Egypt (Coptic), Ethiopia, Syria (Orthodox), Armenia, and some groups in India took this line. However since the 1960s, ecumenical outreach across the fault lines has made progress in repairing ancient breaches. Dorothy Wendebourg states:

> Ecumenical dialogues between the Chalcedonians and Orientals have led to the conclusion that the Christological problems between the two sides have been solved . . . and that the continuation of the separation can no longer be justified on Christological grounds.[72]

Nevertheless the fact remains that ancient anathemas remain in place, and agreement as to the status of ancient councils remains elusive. Western Christians have regarded the Oriental Orthodox and the Nestorians as heretical for 1,500 years, and vice versa.

This complicated history raises an interesting question. Does art produced by churches that had been drummed out of the Roman Empire and regarded as heretical really count as Christian art? If churches are in

---

71. For a summary of these issues and how they stand in modern times, see Wendebourg, "Chalcedon in Ecumenical Discourse,"
72. Ibid., 314.

theological disagreement, what does that mean for the mutual reception of their art? My answer is that art has a value that transcends dispute in regard to theological propositions. People who fight over doctrine can nevertheless be united in their veneration of art. The word divides in a way that images do not, as Mary Charles Murray argues cogently. She gives examples of how art reached across theological boundaries even in ancient times. For instance, at Christmas followers of a "monophysite" theologian waited until after a Chalcedonian group had finished their celebration, and then proceeded to venerate the same image of the Virgin. In another case, after a long day of theological argument, exponents of different traditions both kissed the same Gospel book and the icons. She adds:

> As a matter of historical fact, the artistic expression of doctrine seems to have been the only unifying theological force in the early church. . . . Of its nature art can convey the truth inclusively, and so is much more suited to the expression of orthodoxy as *truth* rather than orthodoxy as *formula*.[73]

A second point in favor of the art of Oriental and Nestorian Christians is that their communities have been terribly ravaged by persecution. They have given their witness to Christ with their blood, and this gives their art a particular value that should be taken into account by Western Christians, who on the whole have suffered less.[74] Therefore, I am perfectly content to include Christian images of art from churches that have not accepted all the Councils that Western Churches have, and would urge readers to do the same. The leaved cross motif attests to the enduring value of a Gospel couched in terms of a Life-Giving Tree. We turn next to further examples of this motif.

---

73. Murray, "Artistic Idiom and Doctrinal Development," 290–92. This article has a comprehensive survey of the issues and interrelationships of word and image, and is warmly recommended.

74. There is more on this theme in chapter six.

An Armenian Khachkar

I am especially fond of the monumental carved cross form of Armenia, called the khachkar, which translates simply as "cross-stone." An article comparing them to Irish High Crosses first piqued my interest in crosses of the first millennium.[75] Seeing them in person is a mesmerizing experience. Khachkars are exquisitely beautiful creations, and the landscape of Armenia is full of them; by one estimate there are 40,000 in the contemporary nation of Armenia, a land only the size of the state of Maryland. Khachkars are regarded as national treasure, and as a symbol of the Armenian soul. Yet they are almost unknown to other Christian communities.

No doubt the general lack of familiarity with this religious art form reflects the overall isolation of Armenia itself. The Armenian language is a member of the Indo-European family but is not closely related to any other of its members.[76] The alphabet is equally opaque to foreign visitors. Large portions of historic Armenia have been absorbed into the modern state of Turkey, and the remainder was a Soviet Republic for seventy grueling years, cut off from the outside world—an experience from which the nation is still in recovery. However, for our purposes the Armenian Church is highly important for two reasons: its antiquity and its devotion to the Cross. Armenia was the first nation to convert to Christianity, preceding the Roman Empire by a decade or more. It has had a continuous existence as a Christian nation of more than 1,700 years, and thus is almost uniquely suited to serve as a link with ancient tradition. In addition to pride in their history, the Armenians boast of their devotion to the Cross, saying that in no other branch of Christianity does the Cross enjoy the prestige that it does among them. Thus, for example, the priest who gives the sermon on Sundays holds a small cross in his hand while he preaches. The Gospel itself is symbolized by the

---

75. Richardson, "Observations on Christian Art in Early Ireland, Georgia and Armenia."
76. Chase O'Flynn, scholar of linguistics, personal communication with author, May 2016.

cross he holds, which, incidentally, is wrapped in a beautifully embroidered silk cloth, as a sign of further piety.

According to scholar Hamlet Petrosyan, khachkars were introduced "in the ninth century CE and were continuously produced until late in the eighteenth century, having reached their aesthetic peak as a form of stone carving in the twelfth and thirteenth centuries, when all Armenian cultural life was flourishing. Following a hiatus during the last two hundred years, they began to reappear late in the twentieth century."[77] New khachkars that are completely faithful to tradition are being carved today. New churches built after the Soviet period feature crosses that are strikingly similar to those carved a millennium ago—subject to the proviso that each khachkar, like a snowflake, must be unique. The overall motif is fixed, but the individual instance is one of a kind. Some khachkars are

A khachkar from a field in Noraduz, Armenia, where some 1,500 of these beautiful carved stone crosses have stood in the open air for centuries. (Credit: author.)

---

77. Petrosyan, "The Khachkar or Cross-Stone." 60.

found in cemeteries, but their primary use is not to mark the graves of the dead. Rather, created as acts of individual piety, they decorate churches and monasteries, commemorate important personages, or honor particular events. No one motive explains all khachkars, which is why they may be found pretty much anywhere: standing in a field, decorating the walls of a church, or keeping sentinel at a monastery.

Formally, khachkars are of the "leaved cross" type. They are flat plinths carved on only one side, and typically have three zones: a bottom level (which usually includes a round shape representing the earth) is for the lower realm, an upper tier connotes the heavens, and the cross in the middle zone joins the two. A vegetative motif comes forth from the base of the cross and curls upward, with tendrils reaching toward the arms. The tips of the cross are trefoil, suggesting buds of new life at the end of each arm, and rich clusters of grapes frequently sprout amid the arms, and catch the eye with their burgeoning growth. The Tree of Life symbolism is abundantly evident. Decorative rosettes and interlace complete the program, sometimes with an intricacy and delicacy that is all but unbelievable. The master carver Poghos in the thirteenth century earned the sobriquet "the embroiderer" for his skill because the patterns he carved were so complex. Our tour guides in Armenia informed us that Poghos worked on individual khachkars for as long as a year. The volcanic tufa from which the crosses are carved lends itself to such delicacy. The tufa is soft enough to work but is surprisingly durable, so that centuries of weathering out-of-doors have caused but little deterioration.

Hamlet Petrosyan explains the origins of the khachkar form as an attempt by the Armenian Church to present the Gospel in a manner consistent with traditional notions. The idea that the world is a garden created by God was popular in Armenia. This makes sense given that grapes appear to have been cultivated there as early as the fifth millennium BCE. Imagery focusing on the Cross as the locus of death and suffering would not have appealed to the sensibilities of the people, he contends, and so,

priests began to speak of the cross as an all-bearing tree sheltering the whole earth, or as a winepress on which divine grapes were
pressed. . . . The cross itself, originally a square shape with four
equally long arms, began to lengthen and was transformed into a
fruit-bearing tree rising from and covering the whole earth, with
pomegranates and clusters of grapes decorating its upper region.
The combination of old and new symbols appeared enticingly alive
and inviting.[78]

Along with the Armenian Church itself, the khachkar form has
helped to maintain cultural identity in a population that has frequently
been beleaguered. One episode in which an alternate cross form was
tried, but failed to achieve acceptance deserves mention. In the thirteenth century, clergy influenced by Western models began commission-
ing khachkars with the body of Christ portrayed as dead or dying. In the
example shown Christ's head slumps forward and his arms hang loosely.
This is called the "All-Savior" cross stone. However, as sometimes happens with innovations imposed from above, Petrosyan notes such crosses
though "outstanding as sculpture . . . have never achieved popularity." [79]

In modern times new styles have been tried in a freer artistic vein.
Traditional skills of carving are being put to use in a more contemporary
mode. Whether these experiments will last longer than the "All-Savior"
model of the Middle Ages remains to be seen. However as another new
example demonstrates, for traditional purposes such as standing guard
in front of a church, something very traditional is still what is desired.
The Life-Giving Tree is alive and flourishing in today's Armenia.

The Sanctuary Curtain at Holy Etchmiadzin

Before leaving Armenia, another image is worth sharing. It is not a Cross,
but it certainly does feature a most life-giving tree. The sanctuary curtain
found in the Cathedral of the primate of the Armenian Church—whose

---

78. Ibid., 62.
79. Ibid., 67.

title is "Catholicos"—depicts what can only be considered a scene of Paradise. This curtain is found at Holy Etchmiadzin, the spiritual center of Armenian Christianity. Like the Coptic curtain considered earlier, it serves to separate the clergy from the people at various points in the liturgy. When it is drawn across to cover the sanctuary, the people can no longer see what is going on behind the curtain, although they can hear the continuous chanting and have the design of the curtain to occupy their visual field.

Remarkably, the Etchmiadzin curtain has a motif virtually identical to the Oued Ramel baptistery floor. Urns flanked by peacocks on either side are the center of attention. A graceful tree rises from each urn, bearing flowers and songbirds upward. If it were the Tree of Life itself, this tree springing up from the urn could give no more delight to the eyes than it does. Elegant columns frame three arches, from atop which descend oil lamps, and from above which seraphim look on with

A rare "All-Savior" type khachkar from Armenia, depicting the crucified Christ. This style never achieved popular acceptance in Armenian Christianity. (Credit: author.)

interest. If one were to try to connect this visual scene with the liturgical action going behind it, the only conclusion could be that our worship is Paradise now.

As a typical Western Christian, I was quite startled the first time I saw a curtain drawn across the sanctuary to divide the clergy from the people. The people must feel left out, like second-class citizens, I assumed. However, the congregation did not seem troubled at all. They sat quietly, listening to the singing of the choir and, if anything, seemed to appreciate a respite from active involvement in the liturgy. Whatever labors the clergy were undertaking on the other side of the screen were presumably for the benefit of all, so the people in the pews could afford to be patient. In time, and with further exposure to the custom, I began to enjoy the periods when the curtain was closed. They are peaceful and meditative moments amid a very active liturgical drama. They also give one an opportunity to muse on the imagery on the curtain, which is quite delightful. Besides, at other times in the Armenian liturgy the clergy

A modern carving with very traditional khachkar design graces the exterior of a new church in Dvin, Armenia. (Credit: author.)

The sanctuary curtain at the Cathedral in Etchmiadzin, Armenia, the seat of the Catholicos. (Credit: author.)

parade through the congregation, chanting, and grinning at people they know, so it is hard to feel left out.

An Ethiopian Processional Cross

The African land of Ethiopia boasts a proud and ancient Christian lineage. King Ezana converted to the new faith only a few years after Constantine, about 324 CE. Coins with an image of the Cross appeared shortly thereafter.[80] Due to the vicissitudes of history and climate, comparatively little art remains from antiquity. However, we do know that art and Christian practice were inseparable in ancient times.[81] Marilyn Heldman comments:

> The sixth century was the period when specifically Christian style and iconography was introduced to Ethiopia. . . . A group of

80. Munro-Hay, "Aksumite Coinage," 101–16.
81. Mercier, *Ethiopian Art History,* 45.

fourteenth century Ethiopian Gospel manuscripts follows the iconography of pilgrimage sites in Jerusalem known from sixth century
pilgrim ampullae.[82]

Thus it is a reasonable inference that Christian art from later periods is in
continuity with earlier creations and reflects their iconography.

A good case in point is a beautiful processional cross now in the
collections of the Walters Museum in Baltimore. Dated to the twelfth to
thirteenth centuries CE, it is much later in origin than some of the other
objects we have considered. However, its vegetal motifs, particularly the
rooting structures at the base of the cross, place it alongside the other
leaved crosses mentioned above. The description provided by Curatorial
Fellow C. Griffith Mann deserves to be quoted in full:

> The complicated design of this cross must have presented a con-
> siderable challenge to its creator, who cast its body in one piece.
> Simple incised borders sharpen and distinguish the individual

*A cast bronze processional cross
from Ethiopia. Image credit: Walters
Museum, Baltimore, MD.* (Credit: Used
according to Creative Common Zero: No
Rights Reserved policy.)

---

82. Heldman, "The Heritage of Late Antiquity," 119.

components of the object. These lines, which were probably added freehand, provide a texture that animates the surface of the entire cross. The numerous perforations create an intricate silhouette, but also serve the practical function of conserving material and minimizing weight. The shaft, perhaps a later addition, was riveted to the base. The foliate decoration of the cross, which simultaneously suggests birds and vegetation, creates a complex pattern around the small cross at the center. In Ethiopian art, birds often serve as heralds of the Resurrection, and their evocation here is therefore appropriate. The multiple projections further strengthen the allusion to the rejuvenating power of the cross, as their tendril-like repetition conveys a sense of organic growth. The additional presence of three smaller crosses at the terminal points of the object reiterates this idea; the crosses spring like young buds from their supporting extensions."[83]

A Cross from the Indian Orthodox Tradition

The original churches of India are if anything even less well known in the West than that of Armenia, and if tradition is to be believed, even more ancient: they claim to have been founded by none other than the Apostle Thomas in 52 CE. He is said to have preached in India, converting kings and commoners, before meeting a martyr's death. Thomas's relics are thought to have been preserved into modern times, and their translation to a new site is the occasion for the feast date of July 3 in the Roman Catholic Church. Though the evidence for Thomas's missionary activity is not of the kind that would convince scientifically oriented historiographers, neither is it impossible that he arrived as claimed. As we noted earlier, in ancient times people could get around and travel long distances if they wished. Certainly the character of Thomas as presented in the Gospels is of a very determined man. He once urged his colleagues to accompany Jesus to die with him, and after receiving the evidence of the resurrection that he boldly insisted upon, immediately came to

---

83. Mann, "The Role of the Cross in Ethiopian Culture," 78.

belief. If any of the apostles could have completed the long journey to lands of strange speech, Thomas is the one.

The history of the ancient churches of India is fascinating but too complex to enter into here. Suffice it to say there are about seven million adherents all told, and that they have fashioned a distinctive national cross form of the leaved type. The example shown here is from yet another sanctuary curtain, used by an Indian Orthodox congregation that the author stumbled upon in Dublin, Ireland.[84] Like the Armenian crosses, this one has trefoil buds at the end of each arm, suggesting new growth. It also has a very clear vegetative structure rising up from the base, with leaves at the bottom and ripe grain sprouting forth at the top. A simple jewel at the crossing gives a hint of the *crux gemmata* form previously encountered, but the predominant emphasis of this cross is of the Living Tree variety.

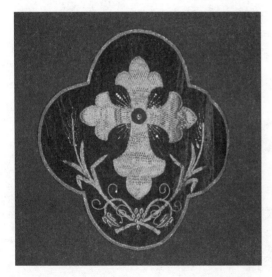

Close-up of a leaved cross design on the sanctuary curtain of an Indian Orthodox congregation in Dublin, Ireland. (Credit: author.)

84. Connections between Irish worship traditions and those of the Oriental Orthodox may be closer than one would suspect. Hilary Richardson has proposed that the famous sixth-century Irish saint Columba travelled with a flabellum, or liturgical fan. These fans are no longer used in Western Christian circles but were very much in evidence at the Indian Orthodox service I attended. See Richardson, *Remarks on the Liturgical Fan, Flabellum or Rhipidion.*

A number of carved crosses of the same general form are extant in India. Although it is not clear in each case how old they are, some are certainly several centuries old at the least. Some of the Indian crosses show a noteworthy attempt to assimilate a traditional design to local tastes: the flowering structure is that of the lotus plant, which is very much a part of Indian culture and religion. Thus, unlike the claim that Irish crosses are sun symbols to appeal to pagans, the lotus crosses may well have been so designed as to seem familiar in a land so influenced by Hindu religion.[85]

A Tibetan Petroglyph

Our last example is from a location perhaps the most unexpected of all, a high mountain pass in the Ladakh region of Tibet. This area along with much of Asia was evangelized by Nestorian missionaries in the first millennium, with considerable success overall. The story is told by Philip Jenkins in *The Lost History of Christianity,* and the extent of the Church of the East is truly surprising.[86] Dioceses in great number stretched right across Central Asia. Monasteries and seminaries sprang up, and pilgrims travelled from as far as China to see the holy places and Jerusalem. Of all the ancient churches formed out of theological controversy farther west, the Nestorian Church of the East has suffered the worst reverses. Successive waves of invaders wreaked havoc and destruction. Today there are only about 40,000 adherents, most of them in the United States and in England. However, back in the day their influence was immense.

One of their number left a carved inscription in the Sogdian alphabet, which reads as follows, "In the year 210 (Arab calendar, corresponding with 825 CE) we sent Caitra from Samarkand together with the monk Nosfarn as messengers to the King of Tibet."[87] Nearby are three crosses,

---

85. Antony, M. Thomas, "Saint Thomas Cross—A Religio Cultural Logo of Saint Thomas Christians," October 9, 2010, http://www.nasrani.net/2010/10/09/saint-thomas -cross-a-religio-cultural-logo-of-saint-thomas-christians/.
86. Jenkins, *The Lost History of Christianity,* 45–70.
87. Thiry, August, "Christian Crosses in Little Tibet," August 14, 2008, website Shlama Mechelen, http://www.shlama.be/shlama/content/view/214/180/.

one of which has been redrawn for ease of viewing. This too is of the leaved cross type. Although the design is very simple and scratched into stone, it clearly shows a branching structure coming up from below, reaching toward the cross arms. Though little is known for certain about other examples of Christian art produced in Central and South Asia in the first millennium, this one is suggestive. Apparently the leaved cross motif was so indelibly present in the mind of the monk Nosfarn and his colleagues that even though the pass was remote and the temperature no doubt bitter, it was worth his while to carve it in full. In the mind of the monk Nosfarn, the Cross and the Life-Giving Tree were, it would seem, one and the same, and the message of the Cross was that of a renewed creation.

Going Deeper

- Select one of the images from this chapter and spend time with it in prayer. Imagine what it would have been like to experience the image in its original setting. In what ways does it open the mystery of Christ?
- Some of the imagery may have been unfamiliar to you. On a simple emotional level, how do you feel looking at these early crosses? Are any of them disturbing or upsetting? Are any particularly

An artist's redrawing of a ninth-century cross incised on a boulder in the Ladakh region of Tibet. (Credit: Aidan O'Flynn.

enlivening? If so, what does this suggest to you about your current spiritual situation?

- The St. John Lateran mosaic shows the effects of salvation in a very lively manner, via the small figures at the bottom enjoying themselves in the River Jordan. Are you able to identify with them? Why or why not? What are they doing in the picture anyway?
- Locate the translation of the runic poem in the Ruthwell Cross section, and read it aloud slowly, while also meditating on the vine-scroll imagery. How do the deeply moving words and the exuberant foliage mutually illuminate one another?

3

Scriptural Connections

Their delight is in the law of the L*ORD, and they meditate on his law day and night. They are like trees planted by streams of water, bearing fruit in due season, with leaves that do not wither; everything they do shall prosper.*

—Ps 1:2–3, Book of Common Prayer

The objects we saw in the previous chapter ultimately derive from a specific historical context. In chapter one we learned more about that context—the great Christian commonwealth of antiquity with Jerusalem at its center. The art of that era comes alive in its meaning when we remember that setting, which early believers took for granted. However, these objects also reflect a tradition of scriptural interpretation. They seem to make reference to certain key passages from the Bible. The frequent repetition of iconographic themes in this art indicates a degree of shared understanding of how those passages should be depicted. Perhaps we could say that the iconography reflects a kind of visualized *Lectio Divina*—divine reading—whereby a process of rumination and meditation on Bible passages was captured in visual art. Our own appreciation of the art will be enhanced if we reflect on those same passages ourselves. If we go through our own process of spiritual digestion, our appreciation of both the art and the Scriptures will be deeper. In this chapter we will look carefully at several Bible passages that seem to be behind the art we have been viewing. Then I will make suggestions for using them in our own process of holy rumination.

In the Beginning: The Tree of Life in Genesis

And the LORD God planted a garden in Eden, in the east; and there he put the man whom he had formed. Out of the ground the LORD God made to grow every tree that is pleasant to the sight and good for food, the tree of life also in the midst of the garden, and the tree of the knowledge of good and evil. A river flows out of Eden to water the garden, and from there it divides and becomes four branches. The name of the first is Pishon; it is the one that flows around the whole land of Havilah, where there is gold; and the gold of that land is good; bdellium and onyx stone are there. The name of the second river is Gihon; it is the one that flows around the whole land of Cush. The name of the third river is Tigris, which flows east of Assyria. And the fourth river is the Euphrates. The LORD God took the man and put him in the garden of Eden to till it and keep it. And the LORD God commanded the man, "You may freely eat of every tree of the garden; but of the tree of the knowledge of good and evil you shall not eat, for in the day that you eat of it you shall die." (Gen. 2:8–17)

Then the LORD God said, "See, the man has become like one of us, knowing good and evil; and now, he might reach out his hand and take also from the tree of life, and eat, and live forever"—therefore the LORD God sent him forth from the garden of Eden, to till the ground from which he was taken. He drove out the man; and at the east of the garden of Eden he placed the cherubim, and a sword flaming and turning to guard the way to the tree of life. (Gen. 3:22–24)

The word for garden in Hebrew is "*gan.*" It refers to a pleasure garden of the sort planted by kings.[88] In the arid Near East, monarchs would create such gardens both as displays of wealth and power, but also

---

88. Rabbi Dena Bodian, personal communication with author, March 2017.

for their practical use as places of recreation and shade in the heat of the day. The celebrated gardens of Babylon were a wonder of the world. The more recently rediscovered gardens of Nineveh used a sophisticated pump system to raise water to rooftop level, water that had already been conveyed many miles by canals from the mountains. So contrary perhaps to many imaginings, the original Eden was not a wilderness. The Sierra Club would be disappointed, but Paradise was not the great outdoors. It was a highly cultivated setting that required a talented cultivator to maintain. Adam and Eve were the cultivators and their assigned task was to "till and keep" the garden.

Several features of the *gan* in Eden would make it stand out, however, even in comparison with humanly devised wonders like the Hanging Gardens of Babylon. Unlike ordinary human gardens, which require water to be brought from a distance, the LORD God's garden was actually a *source* of fresh water. Verses 10–14 tell us, "A river flows out of Eden to water the garden, and from there it divides to become four branches." The branches are the Pishon, the Gihon, the Tigris, and the Euphrates. These four rivers, not all of which are securely identified, are presumably principal water sources of the Near East. The life-giving quality of Eden is suggested by its outflowing waters, a theme that Christian writers and artists would draw upon in due course.

A second remarkable feature of the garden is the presence within it of not one, but two unique trees. Along with planting "every tree that is pleasant to the sight and good for food"—something any earthly monarch could aspire to—the Lord God made to grow "the tree of life also in the midst of the garden" and "the tree of the knowledge of good and evil." These two very special trees could only have been planted by God. Humanity has come to know the latter, the tree of the knowledge of good and evil, only too well. Good and evil are strangely mixed in life and we might well wish we had never learned to taste the difference. The former tree, the tree of life in the midst of the *gan*, humanity did *not* taste. In fact, it was to prevent us from eating of the tree of life and so living forever that God expelled us from Eden. A metaphor for the fallen human condition—our temporary existence of good mixed with evil—is elegantly set forth in these simple verses.

But how are we to understand that mysterious tree in the midst of the garden? The Tree of Life is introduced so casually and without explanation that it must have been a well-known concept, one widely understood in ancient culture. Art historian Jennifer O'Reilly explains:

> The ancient Near Eastern image of the Tree of Life was of a cosmological tree, rooted in the netherworld, the trunk passing through the centre of the earth, its branches reaching to the heavens and supporting the constellations, its fruit offering healing and immortality.[89]

The Tree of Life seems to be extreme shorthand for the source of life itself. It is a prescientific concept, explaining the presence of life everywhere in the known world. The fact that to this day scientists assert the indubitable presence of life elsewhere in the universe offers implicit support for the ancient confidence that life is somehow primary. A cosmos without life is apparently unthinkable, then and now. By co-opting a notion already extant in ancient cultures, and alive in new ways in our own, the biblical authors claimed life's ubiquity for God.

A third noteworthy feature of Eden is the implied relationship among the different personages who appear in the story. There are relationships on three levels: between God and humans, between God and other living beings, and between humans and other living beings. There are also hints of relationship within the divine being—"God said, 'See the man has become like one of us,'"—and within the community of human beings—represented by the first man and the first woman. It would appear that in all these levels of relationship there was at first intimacy, knowledge, and cooperation. Adam and Eve were in the habit of conversing with God when the Lord walked in the garden in the cool of the evening. This is implied by the notice God took one day when they

---

89. O'Reilly, "The Trees of Eden in Medieval Iconography," 170.

did not appear. Previously they must have been regular interlocutors with God, and that is why their nonappearance stood out. Furthermore, humans and animals have ordered relationships, symbolized by Adam and Eve's naming of the various species.[90] Humans also have a relationship of mutual interdependence, as Adam and Eve were created to be partners to one another. So in the first Paradise, humans at first enjoyed intimacy with God, with creation, and with one another. Indeed, intimacy on all these levels is a good working definition of what Paradise really could mean.

Being driven out of Paradise, then, brought strife and separation on all three levels. The earth now provides food only with sweat and pain, men rule over women and siblings quarrel, and the cherubim keep us at bay with a fiery turning sword. As an image of the fallen human situation, this multitiered exile is brilliantly conceived. If restoration of human access to Paradise is the implied work of Christ in the art we have been examining, the story of Genesis 2–3 helps give that work greater specificity. In Christ, strife and separation are overcome: the reversal of exile and restoration of intimacy constitute atonement in the art we are examining.

Leaves for Healing: Ezekiel's Vision of Water and Temple

Then he brought me back to the entrance of the temple; there, water was flowing from below the threshold of the temple toward the east (for the temple faced east); and the water was flowing down from below the south end of the threshold of the temple, south of the altar. Then he brought me out by way of the north gate, and led me around on the outside to the outer gate that faces toward the east, and the water was coming out on the south side.

Going on eastward with a cord in his hand, the man measured one thousand cubits, and then led me through the water; and it was ankle-deep. Again he measured one thousand, and led me through

---

90. The command to rule over other species is not in this version of the creation story, but appears in Genesis chapter one.

the water; and it was knee-deep. Again he measured one thousand, and led me through the water; and it was up to the waist. Again he measured one thousand, and it was a river that I could not cross, for the water had risen; it was deep enough to swim in, a river that could not be crossed. He said to me, "Mortal, have you seen this?"

Then he led me back along the bank of the river. As I came back, I saw on the bank of the river a great many trees on the one side and on the other. He said to me, "This water flows toward the eastern region and goes down into the Arabah; and when it enters the sea, the sea of stagnant waters, the water will become fresh. Wherever the river goes, every living creature that swarms will live, and there will be very many fish, once these waters reach there. It will become fresh; and everything will live where the river goes. People will stand fishing beside the sea from En-gedi to En-eglaim; it will be a place for the spreading of nets; its fish will be of a great many kinds, like the fish of the Great Sea. But its swamps and marshes will not become fresh; they are to be left for salt. On the banks, on both sides of the river, there will grow all kinds of trees for food. Their leaves will not wither nor their fruit fail, but they will bear fresh fruit every month, because the water for them flows from the sanctuary. Their fruit will be for food, and their leaves for healing." (Ezek. 47:1–12)

The people of the Holy Land, ancient as well as modern, are neighbors to a geographical feature that is a byword for sterility: what we call the Dead Sea, and the Bible calls the Arabah. This deservedly famous body of water marks the lowest point on earth. It is part of the same tectonic gash in the earth as the Rift Valley of Kenya. Water enters the Dead Sea from the River Jordan to the north and then has nowhere else to go. It slowly evaporates, leaving behind a pool of water, which over time has achieved enormous salinity. Oddly enough, understanding this curious body of water is helpful in understanding early cross imagery because the Dead Sea is featured in a passage of Scripture that is in the background of certain cross images. Ezekiel's vision of water surging forth from beneath the Jerusalem Temple, recounted in chapter 47, clearly was an inspiration for the river vistas in the Lateran apse mosaic,

for example. In chapter 47 Ezekiel recounts how he saw water miraculously issuing from the temple and flowing eastward until it reached
the Arabah, that is, the Dead Sea. "This water flows toward the eastern
region and goes down into the Arabah; and when it enters the sea, the
sea of stagnant waters, the water will become fresh" (47:8). Starting as a
very modest current at first, the flow becomes deeper and stronger the
farther it proceeds.

I must confess that I had read this passage many times without
understanding what was meant by "the sea of stagnant waters." I thought
vaguely it must be the Red Sea. It wasn't until I actually visited the Dead
Sea that the light dawned for me. The clue was the presence of a sign for
a location on the Dead Sea called En-Gedi. Our tour group was on the
way back to Jerusalem after a typical tourists' day at Qumran, followed
by the obligatory dip in the Dead Sea to find if we really could float
effortlessly. This visit leaves the tourist with a vivid awareness of how
hot, dry, desiccated, salty, and generally inhospitable to life a terrain can
be. When our bus passed the sign for the exit to En-Gedi, I remembered
having read this name in Ezekiel. When I put two and two together, I
was stunned. This—the Dead Sea—is the "sea of stagnant waters," I
realized. This torrid and deadly environment is the one that, in Ezekiel's
vision, is refreshed by pure temple water to become a kind of Paradise.

When I got back to our hotel in Jerusalem I pulled out my Bible and
re-read these verses:

> Wherever the river goes, every living creature that swarms will live,
> and there will be very many fish, once these waters reach there. It
> will become fresh; and everything will live where the river goes.
> People will stand fishing beside the sea from En-gedi to En-eglaim;
> it will be a place for the spreading of nets; its fish will be of a great
> many kinds, like the fish of the Great Sea. [i.e., the Mediterranean]
> (Ezek. 47:9–10)

What astounded me was the physicality of the vision. The sterility of the
Dead Sea area is . . . how to put it? . . . visceral? tactile? the kind you
won't soon forget? The water seems dead in a way that won't easily be

changed. And yet the waters of Ezekiel's vision, though only spiritual and dreamlike, a kind of essence of holiness that trickles out from the altar of the temple, do the trick. How could such a merely theological concept as living water from a dreamt-of temple so thoroughly transform the Arabah? What kind of water is it that could make the Dead Sea hospitable to "many kinds of fish"?

But there was more. Fish are not the only living things to flourish in Ezekiel's vision. He goes on to add:

> On the banks, on both sides of the river, there will grow all kinds of trees for food. Their leaves will not wither nor their fruit fail, but they will bear fresh fruit every month, because the water for them flows from the sanctuary. Their fruit will be for food, and their leaves for healing. (47:12)

I saw at once how many clues there are that Ezekiel meant to evoke a Paradise-like setting. He hearkens back to the book of Genesis in several ways, beginning with the Genesis-like language *every living creature that swarms will live.* Furthermore, as in Genesis, in Ezekiel humans have dominion over other creatures. In Genesis Adam names them, and in Ezekiel fishermen set nets for them. Water flowing forth from the temple in Jerusalem—which was, as we have seen, identified with the location of Eden—reminds us of the four rivers of Paradise flowing forth from the Garden. The trees with unwithering leaves and unfailing fruit might well remind us of the immortal and life-giving trees at the center of that Garden, and the fact that both leaves and fruit are there for food to be eaten by human beings is also an echo of Genesis: "You may eat of any tree of the Garden."

So Ezekiel imagines a connection between the holiness of the temple and a life-creating power of remarkable freshness. The life-creating power in Ezekiel is water, not a tree, yet the two are closely linked. Without water, trees cannot live. The life of the tree is in the water, in the sap, and conversely the greenness and productivity of trees are a sign that water is nearby. This connection is perhaps best put by Psalm 1—which in turn seems to be in the background of Ezekiel's language:

> They are like trees planted by streams of water, bearing fruit in due season, with leaves that do not wither. (Ps. 1:3, Book of Common Prayer)

The "they" being referred to are persons whose "delight is in the law of the Lord, and they meditate on his law day and night." The psalmist adds, "Everything they do shall prosper." Thus we might gather that the holiness of the temple is related to the life-enhancing effects of fruitful application to the Torah of God. Ezekiel's message is that these effects bring freshness and purity to even the most stale and dried-out situations.

The transition from a tree theme to a water theme is one of the great delights to which the study of early cross imagery invites us. In both Genesis and in Ezekiel, the vitality of trees and of water are interrelated. In the New Testament, the Tree of the Cross gives life through baptism: we appropriate the benefits of Christ's saving death by going down into the waters of life. Ezekiel's amazing vision is a classic instance of this connection, which early Christian artists were happy to evoke in their turn.

One work of Christian art in which the vision of Ezekiel is definitely in the background is the apse mosaic at the Lateran. In that beautiful and complex image, waters come from the base of the Cross rather than from beneath the temple, but it is worth remembering that early Christians felt they had a New Temple, the Church of the Holy Sepulcher, where the wood of the True Cross was safeguarded. Thus it is not too fanciful to connect the living waters coming from the Cross with the living waters coming forth from the temple. The four streams at the base of the Cross are clearly labeled as the four streams of Eden, and the water into which they empty is the Jordan, which as we have seen is the source of the water in the Dead Sea. The real clincher, however, is the scene of the tiny human figures frolicking in the water, including at least one person casting a net. It is difficult to see the whole sequence of water pouring from the Cross down to the Jordan where it creates a park-like setting, and not think of Ezekiel's freshening up of the Arabah.

Spiritual Thirst Quenched: Psalm 42

> As a deer longs for flowing streams,
>   so my soul longs for you, O God.
> My soul thirsts for God,
>   for the living God.
> When shall I come and behold
>   the face of God?
> My tears have been my food
>   day and night,
> while people say to me continually,
>   "Where is your God?"
> These things I remember,
>   as I pour out my soul:
> how I went with the throng,
>   and led them in procession to the house of God,
> with glad shouts and songs of thanksgiving,
>   a multitude keeping festival.
> Why are you cast down, O my soul,
>   and why are you disquieted within me?
> Hope in God; for I shall again praise him,
> my help and my God. (Ps. 42:1–5)

Psalm 42 originally was joined by Psalm 43 to make a single poetic unit. When combined the two psalms have three strophes, each ending in the haunting refrain,

> Why are you cast down, O my soul,
> and why are you disquieted within me?
> Hope in God; for I shall again praise him, my help and my God.

A somber mood is found throughout. A variety of vexing circumstances are hinted at, but in each case the poet finds a way to return in hope to the support of a God who is, at the end, ever faithful.

The connection of these Psalms with cross imagery is, once again, by means of a water motif. The poet compares their spiritual longing to the thirst felt by the deer: "As the deer longs for the water-brooks, so longs my soul for you, O God." The situation of a person in a state of thirst, and the refreshment sought by finding water, not surprisingly, reminded early Christians of the experience of baptism. Thus Psalm 42 has a long association with baptismal liturgies, and the idea of depicting deer quenching their thirst by drinking the waters of life is a very pleasing artistic application. The deer drinking deeply from the rivers of Paradise in the Oued Ramel baptistery, as well as the Lateran mosaic, sets forth most poignantly the condition of the human soul brought to God for transformation.

The theme of thirsting reminds us of other examples in Scripture where the need for water became quite intense. The children of Israel during their wanderings found themselves without water, which Moses supplied by striking a rock with his staff. The prophet Elijah experienced a severe drought, during which the widow of Zarephath cared for him, miraculously preserved with meal and oil that did not run out. Jesus, in John's Gospel, says, "I thirst," from the Cross itself. John says this was to fulfill the Scriptures, which perhaps is meant to recall Psalm 22:15, "My mouth is dried out like a potsherd." Thus, there is ample biblical evidence for connecting the quenching of thirst with meeting a profound spiritual need. The deer drinking deep represent a continuing aspiration of the human psyche. They represent a restored humanity, fresh and alive after a season of alienation from God.

Also noteworthy is the connection with temple worship. When the poet speaks of once again coming to behold the face of God, they mean encountering God in temple worship. This becomes clear when the experience of having gone with the throng in joyful procession is subsequently recalled. The feelings of the ancient Hebrew psalmist, desirous of being in the temple again, might well be compared with those of Sophronius longing to worship once more in the Church of the Holy Sepulcher.

Water Gushing up to Eternal Life: Jesus and the Samaritan Woman

> A Samaritan woman came to draw water, and Jesus said to her, "Give me a drink of water." (His disciples had gone to the city to buy food.) The Samaritan woman said to him, "How is it that you, a Jew, ask a drink of me, a woman of Samaria?" (Jews do not share things in common with Samaritans.) Jesus answered her, "If you knew the gift of God and who it is that is saying to you, 'Give me a drink,' you would have asked him, and he would have given you living water." The woman said to him, "Sir, you have no bucket, and the well is deep. Where do you get that living water? Are you greater than our ancestor Jacob, who gave us the well, and with his sons and his flocks drank from it?" Jesus said to her, "Everyone who drinks of this water will be thirsty again, but those who drink of the water that I will give them will never be thirsty. The water that I will give will become in them a spring of water gushing up to eternal life." The woman said to him, "Sir, give me this water, so that I may never be thirsty or have to keep coming here to draw water." (John 4:7–15)

The delightful story of Jesus's conversation with the Samaritan woman has many dimensions and opens many vistas for meditation. The theme of spiritual thirst found in it is familiar from Psalm 42, considered above, and living or life-giving water recalls the passage from Ezekiel, chapter 47. However, with a more specifically Christian understanding, when we interpret the phrase "a spring of water gushing up to eternal life" as a reference to the gift of the Holy Spirit, the passage from John's Gospel comes alive. The experience of feeling the Spirit's presence and action is compared to the joyful force of living water surging up from below. The identification also helps us make sense of some of the imagery we looked at in chapter two. In the baptistery of Oued Ramel, for instance, the dove of the Holy Spirit is depicted on the floor of the font, at the very place where a baptized person would stand while receiving the three courses of water from above. That would have been a very literal experience of gushing water, symbolizing new life coming through the Spirit. The imagery of the Lateran mosaic gives the same message: the water coursing down the sides of the Cross/Tree of Life into the Jordan River waiting below is water that comes forth from the beak of the dove of the Spirit. The action of the Spirit becomes a gushing stream of life to all the living creatures disporting in its current.

Chapter four of John's Gospel is awash (so to speak) with different meanings of water, literal and figural. At first, Jesus himself is thirsty and tired after a long morning's walk in the hot sun. When the Samaritan woman arrives, he asks her for a drink, meaning of earthly water. When she questions his action in speaking to her, Jesus quickly reverses the situation, and instead of asking for water, he moves to giving: he offers the woman "living water." These lines cohere very well with a comparable teaching in the previous chapter, John 3, where Jesus instructs Nicodemus about spiritual insight. In that passage Jesus compares the Spirit to the wind, which moves freely as it will. Like water gushing forth, wind moves with a will of its own: the essence of divine freedom is thus strikingly proclaimed. The result is freedom to worship, wherever one is: God is Spirit and so may be worshipped anywhere at all, by spiritual persons. The Samaritan woman, at first an unlikely candidate for spiritual insight, becomes energized in the course of her conversation with Jesus. By its end she has become an evangelist herself, introducing Jesus to the other residents of her village.

In John's Gospel the gift of the Spirit is also connected with the Cross. It is while on the Cross that Jesus "gives up" or "hands over" the Spirit to John and Mary standing nearby. The gift is confirmed on the third day, when Jesus breathes on his disciples and says to them, "Receive the Holy Spirit." A close connection between the Cross and the Spirit in early art thus is faithful to the biblical prototype.

Christ the True Vine

I am the true vine, and my Father is the vine-grower. . . . Abide in me as I in you. Just as the branch cannot bear fruit by itself unless it abides in the vine, neither can you unless you abide in me. I am the vine, you are the branches. Those who abide in me and I in them bear much fruit, because apart from me you can do nothing. (John 15:1, 4–5)

We have already noted the fondness of ancient artists for decorating crosses with vines and grapes. Many Armenian khachkars feature ripe clusters burgeoning from the cross branches. The Anglo-Saxon affinity for vine-scrolls, inhabited or not, is very characteristic of their carved crosses such as at Ruthwell. The most obvious referent for the grape motifs is of course the wine of the Eucharist. When Jesus identified his own blood, shed for the salvation of the world, with the blessed cup poured out for many, a connection was established that cries out for artistic representation. What better image for the endlessly renewed gift of eucharistic wine could there be than the rich life-giving vine mentioned in John 15? Apart from the vine there is no fruit, but if we abide in the vine, that is, if we continue as part of the eucharistic fellowship, then we indeed bear much fruit. The joyful upward surge of the Ruthwell vine-scroll captures this motion perfectly.

It is interesting to note that the power of the grape was long understood in the Bible. The first mention of planting vines was when Noah came forth from the ark. His vintage had an unfortunate denouement, when he became drunk. Nevertheless, the appearance of wine as part of humanity's new beginning after the flood—a source of refreshment in daily life—is perhaps a type of the more perfect Cup offered by Christ.

Recurring to the theme of the Tree of Life, whose fruit was denied us at first, might there not also be a suggestion that the Eucharist itself is the fruit that now conveys eternal life? Adam and Eve were cast out of the garden lest they should eat of the fruit of the Tree of Life and live forever. After their sin, death was the consequence. But Jesus freely confers eternal life in the Eucharist, for he says, "Whoever eats of this bread will live for ever" (John 6:51). Holy Communion reverses our ancient exile and restores us to our intended state of life with God. This reality is also suggested by the appearance on crosses of a life-giving vine. The fruit of the Tree of Life is the bread and the wine of the Eucharist: a reminder of Christ's death until he comes, it also enables us to bear fruit, and bear it abundantly, when we abide in God's love.

In the Garden: Jesus and Mary Magdalene

> Now there was a garden in the place where he was crucified, and in the garden there was a new tomb in which no one had ever been laid. And so, because it was the Jewish day of Preparation, and the tomb was nearby, they laid Jesus there. . . . (John 19:41–42)

> Jesus said to her, "Woman, why are you weeping? For whom are you looking for? Supposing him to be the gardener, she said to him, "Sir, if you have carried him away, tell me where you have laid him, and I will take him away." Jesus said to her, "Mary!" (John 20:15–16)

Jesus was not in fact the gardener, he was the Risen Lord. However, this deeply moving account of the first resurrection appearance, like many passages in the Gospel of John, hints at more than is on the surface. The first Adam came to life in a garden; the second Adam (to use Pauline language) was raised to new life in a garden. By taking Jesus to be one who shares Adam's task as gardener, Mary perhaps suggests to us a fulfillment of his humanity, a kinship between Jesus and our first ancestor.

In any event, the presence of a garden near the place where Jesus was crucified should no longer surprise us. We have seen several instances of the conflation of Golgotha with Eden, and as noted earlier, Adam's reputed tomb can be seen by visitors to the Church of the Holy Sepulcher to this day. The Tree of Life was in a garden, and the Gospel of John makes a point of the crucifixion taking place near a garden. However difficult it is to imagine the Crucifixion taking place with bright spring flowers nearby, the same is not true of the Resurrection. Where better for Jesus to make the great mystery of Easter known to Mary, the apostle to the apostles, than amid a fragrant, living array of carefully tended flowers? Paradise created, and yet more wonderfully restored, deserves the loveliest setting human imagination can create, which can only be Eden-like in its beauty.

The theme is visible in some of our works of art. The flowers and palms of Oued Ramel, echoed in the sanctuary curtain of Etchmiadzin, illustrate it. So do the flowers flanking the textile cross on the Coptic sanctuary curtain of the Minneapolis Institute of the Arts. The same theme is suggested more generally in the leafy crosses of the Eastern churches. There cannot be just one living tree: in our imagination one tree always calls for more. The Tree of Life, both in Genesis and in John, grows in the midst of a garden.

All Is New: Creation Language in Paul's Writings

> From now on, therefore, we regard no one from a human point of view; even though we once knew Christ from a human point of view, we no longer know him in that way. So if anyone is in Christ, there is a new creation: everything old has passed away; see, everything has become new! All this is from God, who reconciled us to himself through Christ, and has given us the ministry of reconciliation. (2 Cor. 5:16–18)

This passage does not in itself correspond to any particular iconography of the Cross such as we have been examining. Rather, it could be taken as scriptural warrant for the entire program of images, to the extent that they are artistic attempts to render the foundational mystery of a New Creation in Christ. Everything has been made new: how exactly can one render that insight in visual form? Depicting an instrument of death transformed into a giver of life is an excellent and creative way to render a new reality that is so elusive yet compelling.

It will help to pay careful attention to Paul's exact words. The NRSV employs the phrase "from a human point of view" to translate Greek words that more literally say, "according to the flesh." This term "flesh" or "*sarx*" in Greek is a vexed one, especially in Paul's letters.

It sometimes seems that Paul is blaming everything negative about humanity on our bodies, which can feel unfair to our physical being. We need not enter into that controversy, however, because in this case Paul seems to have something very simple in mind. He is calling attention to the fact that at first Jesus appeared to those who encountered him as a normal human being. He could be touched and heard; he suffered thirst and became weary; he was in every respect part of the created order along with every other human being. That is how we considered him originally, so to say that we "once knew Christ from a human point of view" is not at all theologically troublesome to affirm. The great discovery of Easter is that something strikingly new has occurred, such that our original way of thinking about Jesus is no longer sufficient to the facts.

In his quest to explain what the new reality might be, Paul says, "If anyone is in Christ, there is a new creation." This expression is highly significant for our purposes because it hearkens back to the first creation in the book of Genesis. Just as God spoke and the world as we know it came into being, so now God has acted and a new order of things has come into being. The new creation is distinct from the old creation, but conceptually it is in the same category. There are two creative acts of God: the first gave us Adam and Eve and the original Paradise; the second gives us the Risen Christ and a "new creation."

Any artist wondering how to depict the new creation might well want to draw on images from the first creation. Indeed, what else could an artist do? Depictions that call to mind the original freshness of Eden will serve very well when it comes to evoking the freshness of Easter. One might, for instance, depict a cross in a garden—the very thing we have already seen examples of. It is a paradox that calls the mind into activity as we seek to comprehend the new dynamic at work in Christ. Like the parables of Jesus, which in a similar way stimulate the mind to work out what the kingdom might be like, an image of a life-giving Cross in a garden evokes the very mystery it seeks to depict.

Where does one look in real life for the new creation of which Paul speaks? Paul says the creation happens whenever "anyone is in Christ." What exactly it means to be "in Christ" is also a somewhat vexing question. However we will not go far wrong if we see it as meaning simultaneously an individual relationship of dependence and knowing of Christ, as well as belonging to the Christian community. Someone who prays every day of the week and goes to church on Sunday is most certainly "in Christ." Therefore the new creation of which Paul speaks must be sought in the realm of the individual's spiritual engagement and also our communal life as a eucharistic assembly. The new creative impulse occurs in Christian living, in all its aspects.

That this is so becomes clearer from the context of our short passage. From proclaiming a new creation in which everything old has passed away, Paul moves to an appeal to the Corinthians to be agents of reconciliation. As Christ reconciled us to God, we are to be reconciled to one another, to promote new and healthy relationships among those around us. When persons who have been at odds are restored to right relationship, it is a powerful experience. The story of the Prodigal Son is a classic example: the father and at least one of his sons enter upon a renewed relationship that is moving to hear, even just read aloud. Actually participating in such a process of reconciliation is even more potent: it does indeed seem as though everything is new, and that the barriers which hindered mutual trust hitherto need no longer even be considered to exist. Thus when Paul talks about there being a new creation, it would seem that renewed intimacy with neighbor and with God is what he mostly has in mind.

However, as I said above—while considering Genesis 2—it was precisely the renewal of such intimacy that constitutes "atonement in the art we have been considering." I added, "Restoration of human access to Paradise is the implied work of Christ." This being so, artistic representations of crosses with palms, flowers, and burgeoning grapes, could also be taken as commentary on 2 Corinthians 5.

At the End of Time: The Tree of Life in the New Jerusalem

> Then the angel showed me the river of the water of life, bright as crystal, flowing from the throne of God and of the Lamb through the middle of the street of the city. On either side of the river is the tree of life with its twelve kinds of fruit, producing its fruit each month; and the leaves of the tree are for the healing of the nations. Nothing accursed will be found there anymore. But the throne of God and of the Lamb will be in it, and his servants will worship him; they will see his face, and their name will be on their foreheads. And there will be no more night; they need no light of lamp or sun, for the Lord God will be their light, and they will reign forever and ever. (Rev. 22:1–5)

After the book of Genesis we hear almost nothing more of the Tree of Life until the Revelation to John, at the conclusion of the Christian New Testament. Possible scattered references in Ezekiel and in the Psalms add little to our information about it. It is most striking, therefore, that in his eschatological vision of the New Jerusalem, John describes the Tree of Life anew. One gets the impression that the great Tree has been there all along, biding its time, so to speak, while the drama of salvation unfolded across the centuries. As a symbol of God's patient and immutable purpose of creating life, one could imagine none better. In spite of all the hostile workings of the human spirit, the underlying creative impulse remains secure. However we are to conceptualize the Tree of Life, its enduring quality must be part of the account we give.

Remarkably, however, the Tree is now in the midst not of a garden but of a city. It is in the heavenly city, the new Jerusalem, which has just come down from above. Apparently the heavenly city is in the same location as the Garden of Eden had been at first! Unless the Tree has been relocated, which seems unlikely, the New Jerusalem has appeared where Adam once walked. However, by now the metaphorical conflation of Eden with the old Jerusalem (which was taken so literally by early Christians) should be a familiar concept to readers. That John would place the New Jerusalem in the same location is to be expected. The idea of a threefold colocated appearance of Paradise in the Monza ampulla—at Eden, at Calvary, and in the end times, all in one image—finds further exposition in this passage.

Note also that the river of the water of life, like the four rivers of Paradise in Genesis 2, springs from a fresh source. In Genesis 2, four rivers go forth from Eden to bring water to the surrounding regions; in Revelation 22 the water of life goes forth from the throne of the Lamb to irrigate—among other things—the Tree of Life. We have already noted the close coincidence of living-water imagery with the Cross in art that postdates the composition of the Revelation to John. Thus the passage is an anticipation of a theme that will be explored artistically thereafter.

The clearest biblical parallel for our passage is plainly Ezekiel's vision, which we considered above. In that vision the river flowed from the temple out to the Dead Sea, bringing new life to all the waters that it refreshed. The new life includes leaves on the trees, which are for the healing of the nations in Revelation, and "for healing" in Ezekiel. The new life also includes fruit in both visions.

A theme that is new is the immediacy of grace for the redeemed. There is no longer need for a temple, because God and the Lamb themselves are the source of the healing waters. Worshippers will see the face of the Lamb directly and, as a result, the ancient distinction between day and night is overcome. There is no darkness, only light, for those who have gone through the great ordeals and been welcomed into the New Creation. The first intimacy with God that Adam and Eve enjoyed has been restored *in toto*. Indeed, the hold on redemption afforded the redeemed ones is permanent and unshakeable, as they will reign forever and ever. Christ's work of restoring unity among God, humanity, and the created order is tranquilly and gloriously accomplished.

For Further Reflection

We have inferred a process of *Lectio Divina* to be implied behind the works of art we are considering. That is, certain passages of Scripture seem to have been mulled over in a process of holy rumination, with the result that the art became a kind of commentary on the Scriptures. Now that we have reviewed the principal passages of the Bible that seem to be present in the art, it would make sense to do our own *Lectio* directly with those same passages.

What is *Lectio Divina*? It is an ancient prayer practice that is enjoying widespread revival in our day. It involves slow, attentive reading of a passage of Scripture, in a process of inner apprehension under the guidance of the Holy Spirit. Classically there are four stages to the method. Following prayer for the guidance of the Holy Spirit, the four stages are:

- *Lectio* (Reading): The chosen passage is read aloud slowly, with attention from heart and mind.
- *Meditatio* (Meditation): The passage is considered with active reflection. The mind thinks about its meaning, and in particular how it may be God's word to us in the moment.
- *Oratio* (Prayer): The heart is given freedom to respond in love to what has been understood. This may involve intercession, petition, or other types of prayer, or simply conversing with God.
- *Contemplatio* (Contemplation): When the impulse of *Oratio* has reached its conclusion, then moving beyond our own activity of heart and mind we rest in God. It is a time of listening in tranquility, without expectation, simply being open to God's presence, in whatever manner that may occur.

The process may be utilized once for the entire passage, or it may be repeated several times as an individual word or phrase seems to call for exploration. However, the aim of the method is to arrive at the stage of quiet mindfulness, so if this occurs, there is no need to begin over. It is enough to just to be. The main point is that throughout the time of *Lectio*

Divina the guidance of the Holy Spirit in the moment is to be followed. Thus if it seems right to renew the cycle with its four stages, so be it. If not, *Contemplatio* may continue. When the time available is ended, one prays briefly in thanks, and moves on about one's business.

For further reflection, try using the *Lectio Divina* method with one of the passages quoted earlier in the chapter. In an unhurried manner, go through the four steps. There are eight passages; perhaps one could be read in the *Lectio* mode each day, from Sunday to the following Sunday. Along the way it may be helpful to go back and look at the images again, with one's spirit informed by the process of Holy Reading. Ideally this will make both art and Scripture come alive. Is that in fact your experience?

4

A Brief History of Holy Cross Day

Indeed, this cross of inanimate wood has living power, and ever since its discovery it has lent its wood to the countless, almost daily prayers of men.

—Paulinus of Nola, *Epistle* 31.6[91]

The point in the Church's life that is most clearly connected to the Cross and its meaning is the feast of the Exaltation of the Holy Cross, September 14. The focus on this day is the Cross itself, separated (at least in thought) from the narrative aspects of Jesus's passion that are at the forefront in Holy Week. Thus, to review the ways in which this feast has been and is celebrated in the Christian world, both East and West, will clarify and underscore the story we have been telling.

It would be fair to say that today the Exaltation has a higher profile in Eastern churches than in the Western churches. For the Roman Catholic and Anglican traditions in the West, Holy Cross Day is one holy day out of many. In the Greek Orthodox Church, however, the Exaltation is one of twelve great feasts, and has the same liturgical standing as Christmas or Pentecost (Easter being in a class by itself as the Feast of Feasts). In the Armenian Church, the Exaltation is even more privileged, being one of only five major feasts.

---

91. Quoted from Jensen, *The Cross: History, Art, and Controversy*, 49.

It would also be fair to say that the Eastern churches have preserved more of the spirit of the early imagery we have been examining. The original themes—archaic in the positive sense—such as the reopening of Paradise and the gift of the fruits of immortality, are still very much present in the East. In the West there are echoes of these themes, but they give the impression of being souvenirs of a distant past rather than intrinsic to the message of the feast as observed today.

We should also note that the liturgical action of "lifting up," which is the source of the term "Exaltation," differs from East to West. The Eastern churches have maintained a tradition of lifting up and venerating the Cross on September 14, whereas in the West these more dramatic aspects of worship now occur in the context of Good Friday.

Eastern Liturgies: Greek and Armenian

The title of the feast in the Greek Orthodox Church is "The Universal Exaltation of the Precious and Life-Giving Cross."[92] It is kept as a fast day, even if it should fall on a Sunday, and the liturgical color is dark red. A variety of liturgical actions take place during the course of the day, beginning with Small Vespers.

> Before the beginning of Vespers, the priest puts the Holy Cross on a tray decorated with branches of basil or flowers, and places it on the table of the Prothesis.

Later,

> The priest places the tray with the Cross on his head. Preceded by lighted candles and by the deacon who censes the Cross, he goes to the Holy Table, laying the Cross down on it in the center, the Book of the Gospels being set upright at the back of the altar. A candle is lit and left burning in the sanctuary.

The Cross remains on the Holy Table until the conclusion of the Divine Liturgy.

---

92. The excerpts from the liturgy below come from *The Festal Menaion*, 131–63.

During the Doxlogy the priest puts on all his vestments and stands with incense before the Holy Table, on which lies the Precious Cross, upon a tray with branches of basil or flowers.

A solemn censing and procession to the center of the church follows the Fivefold Exaltation: facing east, then north, then west, south, then east again, the priest asks God's mercy while the choir chants Kyrie Eleison one hundred times for each of the cardinal directions. Next,

> The priest makes two prostrations in front of the Cross and kisses it, after which he makes a third prostration. The Cross is then venerated by the other clergy in order of rank and by all the faithful, each making three prostrations, two before venerating the Cross, and one after.

Finally, at the end of the service, the people come forward to personally venerate and receive basil and a flower from the priest. [93]

The texts that are chanted during the course of the various offices are also of considerable interest. A sampling of them is as follows. First, at Small Vespers:

- The Cross of Christ is exalted today, the life-giving Wood on which was fastened in the flesh He who restores all mankind . . .
- As we behold the Wood of the Cross exalted on high, let us magnify God who was crucified upon it in the flesh . . .
- Hail! Cross of the Lord, divine protection of the faithful, invincible rampart, raising us up from earth . . .
- Come ye, and let us all kiss with joy the Wood of salvation, on which was stretched Christ the Redeemer.[94]

Next, at the Great Vespers:

- The Tree of true life was planted in the place of the skull, and upon it hast Thou, the eternal King, worked salvation in the midst

---

93. Fr. Gregory Mathewes-Green, personal communication with author, 2014.
94. *The Festal Menaion*, 132.

of the earth. Exalted today, it sanctifies the ends of the world, and the Church of the Resurrection celebrates its dedication.

- Divine treasure hidden in the earth, the Cross of the Giver of Life appeared in the heavens to the godly King, and its inscription spiritually signified his victory over the enemy. Rejoicing with faith and love, inspired by God he made haste to raise on high the Cross which he had seen in his vision.[95]

Also at Great Vespers:

- Hail, life-giving Cross, unconquerable trophy of godliness, door to Paradise, succor of the faithful, rampart set about the Church.
- Hail, guide of the blind, physician of the sick and resurrection of the dead. O precious Cross, thou hast lifted us up when we were fallen into mortality.[96]

At Matins:

- In Paradise of old, the wood stripped me bare, for by giving its fruit to eat, the enemy brought in death. But now the wood of the Cross that clothes men with the garment of life has been set up in the midst of the earth, and the whole world is filled with boundless joy. Beholding it exalted, O ye people, let us with one accord raise in faith our cry to God: Thy house is full of glory![97]
- Theotokos, thou art a mystical Paradise, who untilled hast brought forth Christ. He has planted on earth the life-giving Tree of the Cross: therefore at its Exaltation on this day, we worship Him, and thee do we magnify.[98]
- Marvelous wonder! The Cross which carried the Most High as a cluster of grapes full of life is seen today exalted high above the earth. Through the Cross we are all drawn to God, and death has

95. Ibid., 137.
96. Ibid., 139–40.
97. Ibid., 146.
98. Ibid., 151.

been forever swallowed up. O undefiled wood! Through thee we enjoy the immortal fruit of Eden, as we glorify Christ.[99]

Observations

In the Greek Orthodox Church the Exaltation is kept not as a feast but as a fast, and its liturgical color is somber, a deep red.[100] Nevertheless many of the themes that were developed in chapters one and two are still present in the Greek texts, starting with the overall mood of joy and exultation. The Cross is hymned as a source of power, protection, and blessing in its own right. More particularly:

- The references to the history of the finding of the True Cross by Constantine, "the godly king," the vision which "appeared in the heavens," and the excavation of the Cross which "was hidden in the earth." This history is taken at face value and is praised as part of God's saving work.
- The ancient connection of the Exaltation with the feast of the Dedication of the Church of the Resurrection—the Holy Sepulcher—is recalled.
- The conflation of Golgotha with Eden, in that the "Tree of True Life" (the Cross) was "planted in the place of the skull," meaning Adam's tomb. Also note that salvation was "worked in the midst of the earth"—Jerusalem was seen as the center of the world and also the location of the original Paradise.
- The emphasis on the wood itself as life-giving, having been physically touched by Christ. Worshippers now kiss the wood in thanksgiving.
- The power of the Cross to heal and give new life.
- The theme of a new Paradise, reopened so that we now eat of the immortal fruit. Christ is compared to "a cluster of grapes, full of

---

99. Ibid., 153.
100. Fr. Gregory Mathewes-Green, personal communication with author, 2014.

life." The Cross is the "door to Paradise," the effects of exile and death are reversed, and the Cross brings healing (a "physician of the sick").

- The liturgical action of lifting up the Cross to bless the church and the world, and the use of basil and/or flowers to signify the Cross's life-giving abundance.

The Armenian Rite

In the Armenian Church the name of the feast is "The Exaltation of the Holy Cross." It is one of five principal feasts of the Armenian Church, and is observed on the Sunday closest to September 14. The rites as observed in the Armenian Church have much of the same form as those of the Greek Church, but in a characteristically exuberant mode. Notably, the liturgical color of the day is green. As in the Greek Church, the Armenian rite contains a number of liturgical actions, described below.[101]

The following preparations are made prior to the beginning of the Divine Liturgy:

> A sufficient amount of sweet basil sprigs, to be distributed to the congregation, is obtained. A silver tray large enough to hold an altar size cross is covered with the sprigs of basil. The cross is placed (in standing position) on the tray and is generously decorated with basil. The cross is veiled with a fine (translucent) cloth and is sprinkled with rose water at the beginning of the Processional.[102]

The basil cross either remains in the center of the nave or is kept in the vestry during the Divine Liturgy. In either case, following the Divine Liturgy the celebrant and other clergy process to the basil cross and take their place round it. The cross is censed. The Trisagion is said in its Armenian form: "Holy God, Holy and Mighty, Holy and Immortal, you

---

101. *Exaltation of the Holy Cross: Processional and Adoration According to the Rite of the Armenian Church.*
102. Ibid., introduction, page v.

were crucified for us, Have mercy on us." The basil-bedecked cross is then carried in procession. The clergy pause four times to bless the east, the west, the south, and the north.

Then, following the procession, the veneration of the cross takes place. The cross is placed on a table in the chancel, the clergy standing in front of it. The choir sings an ancient hymn, "We Bow Down Before Your Holy Cross." Three times the clergy and choir repeat the hymn while the priest censes the holy cross. Then as the hymn "Glory to the Holy Cross" is sung, the clergy, followed by the people, approach the cross and kiss it and receive sprigs of basil.[103]

Now let us review some of the texts chanted during the processional:

Today on the feast of the renewal of the church in Jerusalem
The sign of the Lord our God appeared in great brilliance.
        O peoples, bless Christ and be glad.
For the rays of the holy life-creating cross
Appeared from the east in sun-lit brilliance, in radiant light.
        O peoples, bless Christ and be glad.
The lord's sign, flaming and terrible, marvelous new wonder,
Appeared from the heavens on Holy Golgotha.
        O peoples, bless Christ and be glad.

You stretched out your spotless arms on the Cross,
        O Christ our God,
And in it gave us the sign of victory. By it preserve our life.
The world-saving outstretched wings of your cross,
        O Christ our God,
You gave to us as a staff of power. By it preserve our life.
You gave life again to him who had died by eating from the
        forbidden tree, by the tree of life. By it preserve our life.

O tree of life, Christ gave you to us as the fruit of life, in exchange
        for the death-bringing fruit. Preserve under your protection the
        assembly of believers.

---

103. Ibid., 24.

Through you the way was opened to us to the tree of life, guarded
by the Seraphim. Preserve under your protection the assembly
of believers.
Through you our first father was delivered from the sin of tasting
the forbidden fruit. Preserve under your protection the assembly
of believers.
And all believers bow down in worship before you. Preserve under
your protection the assembly of believers.

We all bless you for the life-giving Cross,
which became our salvation.
From the Father and light (the cross) arose on earth
with brilliant light
And (was given to believers) as the staff of might
After its wonderful and brilliant appearing it was given us as help
against the enemy. We all bless you for it.[104]

Readings from the Gospels are interwoven into the procession and its
stations.

Observations

The liturgy of the Exaltation is an uplifting multisensory experience. The
fragrance of the basil slowly fills the church during the Divine Liturgy,
mingling with the abundant incense. Worshippers see the bright green
cross, smell its aroma, hear it hymned, and taste the evocative spice, all
of the senses pulling the whole person into a liturgically rich encounter.
The use of green as the liturgical color further highlights the life-giving
quality of the worship.

The texts are, if anything, even more aware of the historical beginnings of cross veneration than are the Greek. The connection with
the rededication ceremonies of the Church of the Holy Sepulcher in
Jerusalem is mentioned specifically. Also of great interest is the recol-
lection of an event recorded in the early days of Christian Jerusalem: a
brightly shining cross appeared in the skies over the Holy City on the day

---

104. Ibid., 12.

of Pentecost in the year 351 CE. It is said to have remained clearly visible for several hours, and caused a sensation at the time. This is the apparent meaning of the verses about the cross appearing "from the east in sun-lit brilliance, in radiant light."

Constantine and his role are not mentioned directly, however. Perhaps this reflects the fact that unlike the Greek Church, the Armenians were only occasional subjects of the Eastern Roman Empire and had something of a love-hate relationship with its various rulers. Still, the early setting of Jerusalem as the home of "the sign of the Lord our God" is clearly remembered and valued.

The theme of Paradise reopened is stated explicitly, as is the gift of the "fruit of life." The Cross is referred to as the Tree of Life, formerly protected by the seraphim but now freely accessible. The Cross is a divine gift in its own right, and a source of power. The Cross is addressed directly, and its protection sought.

As in the Greek rite, worshippers first experience the "lifting up" of the cross toward the four cardinal directions, seeking God's blessing on the whole earth, and then also venerate it in person. They also receive a sprig of basil to taste. Unlike the Greek rite, however, there are no flowers associated with the cross; rather it is itself bedecked with fresh basil, making it look alive.

Western Liturgies: Roman Catholic and Anglican

As mentioned above, liturgical drama associated with the Cross in Western rites occurs on Good Friday, not Holy Cross Day. The latter feast is observed with offices and celebration of Holy Eucharist, but without particular ceremonial. This being the case, it will be worthwhile to take a detour to Holy Week, to see what aspects of Cross ceremonial do occur in the Roman Catholic and Anglican rites on that day.

Good Friday, Roman Catholic Rite

The Roman Missal directs that "The Celebration of the Passion of the Lord" ordinarily take place at about 3:00 p.m. on Friday of Holy

Week. The Celebration consists of three parts: the Liturgy of the Word, the Adoration of the Cross, and Holy Communion. The Adoration in turn consists of two parts: the "Showing of the Holy Cross" and the "Adoration of the Holy Cross."[105]

The Showing has two forms, either of which may be used according to local needs. In the first form, which is the more elaborate, the deacon carries a violet-veiled Cross from the sacristy to the center of the sanctuary preceded by two ministers with candles. The priest receives it there and

> standing before the altar and facing the people . . . uncovers a little of its upper part and elevates it while beginning to sing, "Behold the Wood of the Cross, on which hung the Salvation of the world." When he is finished the people respond, "Come, let us adore." Then, at the end of the singing, all kneel, and for a brief moment adore in silence, while the Priest stands and holds the Cross raised.[106]

The priest then uncovers the right arm of the Cross, and elevates and sings as before. The Showing concludes with the priest uncovering the entire Cross, and elevating it for silent adoration a third time, with singing as before.

For the Adoration proper, the priest hands the Cross to the two ministers to hold. Candles are placed to the right and to the left, after which the

> Priest Celebrant alone approaches, with the chasuble and his shoes removed, if appropriate. Then the clergy, the lay ministers, and the faithful approach, moving as if in procession, and showing reverence to the Cross by a simple genuflection or by some other sign appropriate to the usage of the region, for example, by kissing the Cross.[107]

Three chants are provided as options to be sung while the members of the congregation individually show their reverence. They are, "We adore your Cross, O Lord," the Reproaches, and "Faithful Cross." This

---

105. *The Roman Missal, Study Edition*, 329–36.
106. Ibid., 129.
107. Ibid., 330.

latter hymn is a contemporary version of the sixth-century hymn, "Sing, Tongue, the Battle of Glorious Combat," attributed to early Christian poet Venantius Fortunatus. The contemporary version contains texts of interest to the theme of the life-giving tree, such as the refrain:

> Faithful Cross the Saints rely on,
> Noble Tree beyond compare!
> Never was there such a scion,
> Never leaf or flower so rare.

And from the stanzas:

> For, when Adam first offended,
> Eating that forbidden fruit,
> Not all hopes of Glory ended
> With the serpent at the root:
> Broken nature would be mended
> By a second tree and shoot.

And:

> Lofty timber, smooth your roughness,
> Flex your boughs for blossoming;
> Let your fibers lose their toughness,
> Gently let your tendrils cling;
> Lay aside your native gruffness,
> Clasp the body of your King!"[108]

Good Friday, Anglican Rite (Episcopal Church)

The proper liturgy for Good Friday in the Book of Common Prayer follows the same general pattern as the Roman rite, although ceremonial of the Cross and Communion are both optional.[109] Following the liturgy of the Word the rubrics state:

> If desired, a wooden cross may be brought into the church and placed in the sight of the people. Appropriate devotions may

---

108. Ibid., 333–35.
109. *The Book of Common Prayer*, 276.

follow, which may include any or all of the following, or other suitable anthems.[110]

Three optional anthems are "We Glory in Your Cross, O Lord," "We
Adore You, O Christ," and "O Savior of the World." The rubrics then
specify, "The hymn, 'Sing, my tongue, the glorious battle,' or some other
hymn extolling the glory of the cross, is then sung."[111]

Holy Cross Day, Roman Catholic

Unlike the rituals of Good Friday just described, no particular ceremonial
attaches to the Roman Catholic observance of September 14, other than the
usual actions that attend the Mass. Nevertheless, the texts pertaining to the
feast are well worth consideration for it is in them that the thematic understanding of the feast is expounded.[112] The liturgical color of the feast is red.

Entrance Antiphon:

> We should glory in the Cross of our Lord Jesus Christ, in
> whom is our salvation, life and resurrection, through whom
> we are saved and delivered. (Cf. Galatians 6:14)

Collect:

> O God, who willed that your Only Begotten Son should
> undergo the Cross to save the human race, grant, we pray, that
> we, who have known his mystery on earth may merit the grace
> of his redemption in heaven. Through our Lord Jesus Christ,
> your Son, who lives and reigns with you in the unity of the
> Holy Spirit, one God, for ever and ever.

Offertory Antiphon:

> Protect your people, O Lord, by the sign of the holy cross,
> from the attacks of all enemies; so that our service may be
> agreeable unto you and our sacrifice acceptable, alleluia.

---

110. Ibid., 281.
111. Ibid., 282.
112. *The Roman Missal, Study Edition*, 946–48.

Prayer over the Offerings:

> May this oblation, O Lord, which on the altar of the Cross canceled the offense of the whole world, cleanse us, we pray, of all our sins. Through Christ our Lord.

Preface (The victory of the Glorious Cross):

> It is truly right and just, our duty and our salvation, always and everywhere to give you thanks, Lord, holy Father, almighty and eternal God. For you placed the salvation of the human race on the wood of the Cross, so that, where death arose, life might again spring forth and the evil one, who conquered on a tree, might likewise on a tree be conquered, through Christ our Lord. Through him the Angels praise your majesty, Dominions adore and Powers tremble before you. Heaven and the Virtues of heaven and the blessed Seraphim worship together with exultation. May our voices, we pray, join with theirs in humble praise, as we acclaim: Holy, Holy, Holy Lord God of hosts . . .

Communion Antiphon:

> When I am lifted up from the earth, I will draw everyone to myself, says the Lord. (Cf. John 12:32)

Prayer after Communion:

> Having been nourished by your holy banquet, we beseech you, Lord Jesus Christ, to bring those you have redeemed by the wood of your life-giving Cross to the glory of the resurrection. Who live and reign forever and ever. Amen.[113]

An extraliturgical blessing of basil does also exist:

Almighty and merciful God, deign, we beseech Thee, to bless thy creature, this aromatic basil leaf. Even as it delights our senses, may it recall for us the triumph of Christ, our Crucified King and the power of His Precious Blood to purify and preserve us from evil so

---

113. Ibid.

that, planted beneath His Cross, we may flourish to Thy glory and spread abroad the fragrance of His sacrifice. Who is Lord forever and ever.

The bouquets of basil leaf are sprinkled with Holy Water. (The directions do not state what recipients are to do with their blessed bouquets.)[114]

Observations

The mood of the texts is solemn and inspiring. However, by contrast with the extensive chants of the Eastern churches and their rich typological cadences, the texts feel sparse by comparison. Notably, themes of Paradise and the Tree of Life are absent. Where a tree typology is employed, it is to contrast the wood on which death arose—the Tree of the Knowledge of Good and Evil, not the Tree of Life—with wood on which life conquers. The Cross is called "life-giving," but in the sense of being the locus of Christ's actions rather than a source of power in its own right.

The focus throughout is on Christ's work and dignity, rather than on the Cross as an independent actor. The wood of the Cross is the setting, the "altar" on which salvation was won, but is not itself addressed or hymned as in the Eastern examples.

The effects of salvation in the lives of worshippers are described in general terms: "That we, who have known his mystery on earth may merit the grace of his redemption in heaven."[115] The use of red as the liturgical color ties the feast to Holy Week, for which the color is also red.

Holy Cross Day, Anglican Rite (Episcopal Church)

In the Episcopal Church, Holy Cross Day is ranked as one of many Holy Days that are not principal feasts. However, it is given distinction in two subtle ways. First, along with seven other Holy Days, a proper for an Eve

---

114. "The Blessing of Basil Leaf in Honour of the Holy Cross," Vultus Christi, September 13, 2014, http://vultuschristi.org/index.php/2014/09/the-blessing-of-basil-leaf-in/.
115. *The Roman Missal, Study Edition*, 946.

of the Feast is provided. Second, in the Daily Office, Holy Cross Day shares an antiphon with Epiphany and the Feast of the Transfiguration: "The Lord has shown forth his glory: Come let us adore him." The liturgical color is red. The following texts from the Episcopal Book of Common Prayer indicate the thematic content of the feast.

Collect:

> Almighty God, whose Son our Savior Jesus Christ was lifted high upon the cross that he might draw the whole world to himself: Mercifully grant that we, who glory in the mystery of our redemption, may have grace to take up our cross and follow him; who lives and reigns with you and the Holy Spirit, one God, in glory everlasting.

The Proper Preface is of Holy Week:

> For our sins he was lifted high upon the cross, that he might draw the whole world to himself; and, by his suffering and death, he became the source of eternal salvation for all who put their trust in him.[116]

Observations

The thematic content of the BCP is even more limited than of the Roman Catholic missal; indeed, the same theme is repeated three times in the course of the celebration. The language of the appointed Gospel from John—"For our sins he was lifted high upon the Cross that he might draw the whole world to himself"—is repeated in the collect and yet again in the Proper Preface. This threefold announcing of the theme propounds one idea to the exclusion of others. The response sought in worshippers is that we might take up our cross and follow him. All in all the observance functions as a reminder of Holy Week themes, and does not develop the connections with New Creation that we have seen in the East.

---

116. *The Book of Common Prayer*, 244, 379.

Origins of the Feast

Having sampled the various liturgies of modern churches, and having noted a distinct difference in style of observance between East and West, it will now be useful to review the long history of the Feast of the Exaltation. This will shed light on the origins of these differences. In an invaluable study, Louis Van Tongeren has sifted the available sources from antiquity to establish its probable course.[117]

An inference to be drawn from his work is that the Eastern and Western versions of the Feast as celebrated today may reflect the two different occasions of veneration of the Cross in early Jerusalem. The Western tradition has adopted a ritual derived from the customs of ancient Good Friday, whereas Eastern practice has emphasized the model of what was originally called the Feast of the Dedication, in mid-September. These two observances must therefore be briefly reviewed.

On Good Friday, according to Egeria (ca. 385 CE), "All the people go past one by one. They stoop down, touch the holy Wood first with their forehead and then with their eyes, and then kiss it, but no one puts out his hand to touch it. Then they go on."[118]

On the second day of the festival of the Dedication, that is, on September 14, according to the Armenian lectionary of 415 CE, "the venerable, life-giving and holy Cross was displayed for the whole congregation." The model of displaying the Cross to an entire congregation is what in due course came to be known as the Exaltation, the lifting up of the Cross. "This display or exaltation of the Cross constituted the central ritual element of the feast that developed into the feast of the Exaltation of the Cross," says Van Tongeren.[119] This feast became the basis for the Eastern traditions of the Exaltation as examined earlier. By the ninth century, the Byzantine liturgy for the

---

117. Van Tongeren, *Exaltation of the Cross.*
118. Wilkinson, *Egeria's Travels to the Holy Land*, 137.
119. Van Tongeren, *Exaltation of the Cross*, 37.

Exaltation "appears to have already taken on much of the shape which it retains to this day."[120]

It was, however, the model of humbly kissing the Cross—whether an actual relic or a replica is unknown—that was the form in which a liturgy celebrating the Cross on September 14 was first introduced in Rome:

> The first mention of the feast of the Exaltation of the Cross is in the *Liber pontificalis*, which reports that in a dark corner of the sacristy of St. Peter's Pope Sergius I (687–701) found a cross decorated with costly gems, containing a piece of wood from the Cross of the Lord. The biographer continues, "(that the relic) from that day is venerated with a kiss by the whole Christian population, to the salvation of the human race, and is adored on the day of the Exaltation of the Holy Cross in the basilica of the Saviour, which is also called the Constantinian basilica."[121]

Thus from the beginning what we might call a "Good Friday emphasis" was present in the Western observances on September 14 to a degree it was not in the East. The element of "lifting up" of a cross, which is the central feature of the Eastern observances of the Exaltation, was not employed on the feast of the same name in the Roman West.[122] In time, the ritual of veneration with a kiss was transferred to Good Friday, and dropped out of the Roman observance of the Exaltation, although, as we have seen, Good Friday continued to feature the element of "lifting up."

According to Van Tongeren, when the rite was first introduced in Rome it consisted of a veneration of a cross following the mass for the two saints commemorated on September 14, Cornelius and Cyprian.[123] As in Jerusalem, so too in Rome, the original form of the observance was

120. Ibid., 38.
121. Ibid., 39–40. Van Tongeren argues that the date of the introduction of the feast to Rome predates Sergius and was probably around 630 CE.
122. It is not clear whether the phrase "and is adored on the day" indicates a separate action or simply refers to the previously mentioned veneration "with a kiss." In any event, if the adoration did include a "lifting up," this is not explicit in the early account quoted above.
123. Ibid., 61.

ancillary to a preexisting observance. From this beginning it gradually grew into a feast in its own right, with its own mass-set.

Although the title of the feast in East and West was the same—the Exaltation—thematically the focus diverged early on. In the West, the focus turned to the lifting up of Christ (rather than the Cross) and the feast became a celebration of his role as mediator of salvation. The Cross became the setting, the altar, of his saving work. Speaking of the Western rites, Van Tongeren comments:

> The name (Exaltation) continues to preserve a reference to the oldest element of the feast. Since the expansion of the ritual of the Cross into a fully developed feast with its own formulary, the elevation of the Cross is no longer explicitly a theme in the textual material. What is specific to the feast is not the exaltation, but the Cross. . . . The Exaltation is primarily a commemoration of the Cross, in which the Cross symbolizes Jesus' salvific acts in sacred history.[124]

In the East, however, the focus remained more on the Cross itself and its "universal exaltation"—its being lifted up in every place as a locus of power in its own right.

Nevertheless, even in Rome, and later throughout the Frankish realms and the rest of Western Europe, the themes of the feast were recognizably those of victory and salvation. It may have been Christ who was lifted up and not the Cross itself, but through Christ's exaltation benefits were understood to be conferred on humanity and Paradise was reopened. A typological reading of salvation history was present in the developed form of mass-sets for the Feast, in which the curse of the ancient Tree was reversed in redemption wrought through the life-giving wood. Furthermore, apotropaic powers of averting demonic influence and sin were ascribed to the Cross itself. Thus the sign of salvation continued to be a concrete aid to the Christian, and the Cross was an

---

124. Ibid., 278

effective source of power and holiness in daily life. Despite a difference in practice, the theme of the Cross as a sign of Christ's victory was operative at first in both East and West.[125]

According to Van Tongeren, this theme of victory and glory continued in the liturgy for the Exaltation even after a shift in the meaning of redemption occurred in the West. Under the influence of dominant figures such as Bernard of Clairvaux and Francis of Assisi, the earthly figure of a suffering Christ began to prevail in Europe. The older image of Christ as victorious over death was replaced by a sense of compassion for his painful self-offering. The mass-sets of the Middle Ages, however, did not change to reflect this and failed to keep pace with the times. The liturgical notions of the early Middle Ages remained intact, leading to a disconnect between the worship of the Exaltation and the piety of the times. Van Tongeren comments on this in the final sentence of his magisterial study: "Tradition has perhaps been safely preserved, but since then the liturgy of the Exaltation of the Holy Cross has no longer been a place where the contemporary religious significance of the Cross could be found."[126]

A Modest Proposal

This short survey of the history of Holy Cross Day may leave an overall impression of confusion. Elements from diverse settings have interacted over time so that no single message is given across all the various exemplars of the Feast. This is in contrast to the original situation in early Christian Jerusalem, where two different week-long observances—Holy Week in the spring and the festival of the Dedication in the autumn—offered two distinct liturgical actions that mutually interpreted one another. On Good Friday, as part of Holy Week, worshippers bowed to kiss the wood of the Living Tree in a personal act of devotion and commitment. On September 14, as part of the Dedication festivals, the wood

125. Ibid., 282.
126. Ibid., 284.

of the Living Tree was displayed to the congregation in a more public act of corporate rejoicing.

A modest proposal would be for modern Christians to restore this ancient clarity by observing two liturgies that once again mutually reinforce each other but remain distinct. On Good Friday a personal act of veneration in the presence of the Cross would be the focus; and on September 14, a celebration of the Tree of Life would be the focus. These liturgies would reflect the two different kinesthetic experiences pioneered in ancient Jerusalem. It is one thing to kneel to kiss the wood; it is another to stand in a crowd singing with joy while the saving sign is lifted high. Both have value and both reflect aspects of authentic spirituality. The Good Friday veneration might recall—for instance—the story of the woman weeping at Jesus's feet and drying them with her hair: a telling and intimate avowal of gratitude. The Holy Cross Day exaltation might recall a line from the Psalms: "When the LORD restored the fortunes of Zion, then were we like those who dream" (Ps. 126:1, Book of Common Prayer).

It would be impossible to restore the ancient situation *in toto*. Jerusalem is no longer an exclusively Christian city nor is the Church of the Holy Sepulcher the temple of a Christian world. To the extent that the ancient liturgies were a triumphalistic celebration of a Christianized world, they no longer suit the times. Neither does a dedication festival of the Church of the Holy Sepulcher have much resonance today. For these reasons, a somewhat revised theme for Holy Cross Day in particular is perhaps called for, and a Festival of the Cross as the Tree of Life would be a very suitable candidate. It does seem to have appeal to Christians of our day, and, as has been documented in the preceding chapters of this book, the themes of Paradise and of Living Wood are amply present in the tradition as well.

By way of experimenting with this two-fold observance of the Cross, my Episcopal congregation in upstate New York began keeping Holy Cross Day as a festival of the Tree of Life in 2010—with the bishop's approval. We developed a revised Proper with lessons emphasizing the connection of Tree and Cross.[127] Following the Eucharist we employed an Exaltation ceremony based on the Armenian rite as described above, complete with aromatic basil-bedecked Cross, whose flavorful sprigs were shared with the congregation at the end of worship.[128] We also began to create new liturgical material, based on ancient models but with a more contemporary sensibility. A new hymn text entitled "The Tree of Life," based on my poem of the same name, was a first step.[129]

The Tree of Life

In the beginning you stood in Eden
Loveliest of trees, 'mid fragrant boughs,
Full of bright flow'rs and sweetest fruit of all.
How we longed for life eternal,
Reaching for your fruit in vain.
Finding only death, still forever singing:
Hail gold-green life-giver,
Hail gold-green life-giver!
Amid your branches may we live.

In middle times, your roots were planted
In the flinty rock of Calvary,
Wood and flesh were torn as humans raged at God.
Neither death nor nails could hold Christ.
When He rose, new fruit you bore,
Giving us a taste of paradise and singing:
Hail gold-green life-giver,
Hail gold-green life-giver!
Amid your branches may we live.

---

127. The lessons chosen were a hybrid of Tree of Life texts, and ones already in use for the Prayer Book observance of Holy Cross Day. We used Genesis 2:8–16, Psalm 98, Revelation 22:1–5, and John 3:13–17.

128. A brief video showing the blessing ceremony is available online at https://youtu .be/5kVx7Hwo4Jg. I wish to thank John Bowen for creating and sharing this video, made at St. Thomas's Church, Hamilton, New York, in September 2013.

129. I wish to thank composer Dianne Adams McDowell for her beautiful setting of this hymn text. With her son Mason she has recorded a version that is available on YouTube at https://youtu.be/iphBwzBNIZA.

At the end of time (when we shall see Him)
By the living waters you will grow
Twelve-fold fruits amid your healing leaves.
We await with joyful laughter,
For your saving sign we see:
Though summer fade, Springtime is eternal!
Hail gold-green life-giver,
Hail gold-green life-giver!
Amid your branches may we live![130]

One issue we did not fully resolve is the appropriate color for the liturgy. For Roman Catholics, Eastern Orthodox, and Anglicans, the color employed hitherto is red, which connects the feast with Holy Week. But this would reintroduce an element of confusion, as the whole point of this modest proposal is to keep the Exaltation and Good Friday distinct. Another possibility is to follow the lead of Egeria, who tells us that in early Jerusalem the Dedication "feast ranks with Easter and Epiphany," and that "they decorate the churches in the same way . . . as at Easter and Epiphany."[131] In modern times both of these feasts employ white as the liturgical color for vestments and hangings. Another possibility, even more daring, would be to emulate the Armenian color scheme and also take a leaf from Hildegard's thinking (see chapter five), and choose *viriditas:* green-ness. For Hildegard, greening represents the synergy of Holy Spirit and of created life, and on this basis a green theme for church decoration on Holy Cross Day would be entirely in order. However, in the current Anglican system, green is never a color for feast days, but is used only in "ordinary time." So the color question remains unresolved, and in quest of further discernment.

One last question has to do with the rank of the Feast. As noted above, in ancient Jerusalem the Dedication festival ranked with Easter and Epiphany. For Eastern churches to this day, the Exaltation is one of

---

130. The Tree of Life, copyright 2015 by Donnel O'Flynn and Dianne McDowell, used by permission.
131. Wilkinson, *Egeria's Travels to the Holy Land,* 147

the highest feasts, one of a select group of twelve for the Greek Church, and one of only five for the Armenian. In the Episcopal system, the seven "Principal Feasts" do not, at present, include Holy Cross Day. A rather less modest proposal would be to consider elevating the Feast of the Holy Cross to be an eighth Principal Feast. This proposal would raise some eyebrows and provoke some pointed questions, but that would not necessarily be a bad thing. Looking for answers that work across the entire expanse and experience of Christianity might well ensue.

Going Deeper

- An important aspect of the Greek and Armenian liturgies of the Exaltation is the way they address the Cross directly; for example, "Through you the way was opened to us to the tree of life, guarded by the Seraphim." The Cross is spoken to as though it has life and agency in its own right. Does that make sense to you? How do you respond to the mood of exultation in the Eastern liturgical poetry?
- When athletes are victorious, they elevate the trophy they have won while their fans cheer. Is the Exaltation of the Cross the same as that, or different?
- An old hymn warns believers against "bowing down to wood and stone." Is venerating the wood of the Cross, either on Good Friday or Holy Cross Day, a kind of idolatry? Why or why not?
- What do you make of associating the Cross of Christ so directly with something so earthy and pungent as a sprig of basil?

5

A New Springtime for the Tree of Life

One winter's day he saw a tree stripped of its leaves, and considered that sometime afterward these leaves would appear again, followed by flowers and fruit. He then received a lofty awareness of the providence and power of God that never left him.
—Brother Lawrence, *Practice of the Presence of God, First Conversation*[132]

In Western Christian circles, awareness of the Life-Giving Tree is in a wintry season. After a last flourishing in the Middle Ages, when romantic legends of the Tree of Life circulated, its verdure gave way before the chill winds of Reformation and Enlightenment.[133] Isolated examples in art and poetry are still being created even today, but they do not spring from a living tradition of the church in the way that for instance khachkars do for Armenian Christians. The language of Cross as Tree of Life is not resonant; springtime, if it is to come, is still in the future.

---

132. De Beaufort, *The Practice of the Presence of God*, 61.
133. See Jensen, *The Cross: History, Art, and Controversy,* chapter six, and Irvine, *The Cross and Creation in Liturgy and Art,* for poems, works of art, and theological speculations about the Tree of Life in the Middle Ages and modern times.

The liturgical suggestions in chapter four (if adopted) would be one new green leaf, but many more such leaves will have to sprout before we can really tell how much life remains in the venerable Tree. There would have to be some real contact with modern sensibilities, and some actual practices in daily life, of a kind that support spiritual development for contemporary Western Christians, before we could say the Tree is truly flourishing anew. Looking for such contact and support is the aim of this chapter.

There are reasons for optimism. As we have seen, Eastern Christian liturgies still celebrate the Tree and we can learn from them. Furthermore, moderns are as fascinated by life as any other age: witness the scientific quest for life on other worlds. A theology that associated the mystery of life with the gift of the Cross should find an attentive audience. Nor is this all. I have become aware of two additional and quite potent realities: maybe there really is an *elan vital,* a life energy, of the sort the Tree was created to represent in the first place, and perhaps we can become more aware of this persistent energy. In addition, there is at least one sprout of antiquity that is authentically Western and has been rejuvenated in recent years: the writings of Hildegard of Bingen.[134] I believe she can help connect the Living Tree to modern sensibilities, and also guide us toward actual practice to experience its power in our daily lives. Both of these points can best be explained if we turn our attention first to this remarkable medieval woman.

Hildegard of Bingen lived roughly halfway between antiquity and our own times, so she is well positioned to be a steppingstone between then and now. She used to great effect a term that captures the spirit of the unstoppable power of life itself, a term she did not invent but regularly invoked: the Latin word *viriditas,* which translates into English as "green-ness." But in Hildegard's vision it took on a much greater significance than mere color. In her writings *viriditas* is the color of life itself. It is the freshness of new growth, found in the joyfully bedewed grass,

---

134. For reasons to consider her a "sprout of antiquity," see below.

in verdant trees, in flowers, and even in human beings. If any one term could suggest the life-giving force present in an image so imposing as The Tree of Life, *viriditas* would be it. I would like to begin this survey of Hildegard's thought by referring to the book that first brought *viriditas* to mind in connection with the Tree of Life. I had been wondering whether the life-giving powers associated with that Tree have any real-world efficacy, when a book by Dr. Victoria Sweet came to my attention.[135]

God's Hotel has an actual example of *viriditas* from real life. Published in 2012, it describes Dr. Sweet's work at Laguna Honda Hospital in San Francisco, where she attended chronically ill and impoverished persons. She used this otherwise frustrating setting to experiment with the medical models used by Hildegard. Dr. Sweet was struck that Hildegard discerned *viriditas* to be active in humans as well as in plants. The power in plants to put forth leaves, flowers, and fruits was also claimed by Hildegard to be present in humans as we grow, give birth, and heal. While pondering all this, Dr. Sweet tells us, "I met Terry Becker, who would show me what *viriditas* really meant." Terry Becker was thirty-seven years of age when they met.

> She was a street person, I read in her records, a heroin addict, and a prostitute; she had a boyfriend and they lived on the streets. . . . [She suddenly developed] transverse myelitis, which is an inflammation of the spinal cord that, in just a few hours, can cause a section of the spinal cord to swell . . . devastating to the body's ability to move.

Dr. Sweet had studied the methods of Hildegard and decided to use them on the terrible bedsore that Terry had developed, which had defeated the best efforts of scientific medicine. She decided simply to

> remove obstructions to Terry's *viriditas*, to Terry's natural ability to heal. Because if nothing was in the way, then *viriditas* would heal her wound as surely as a plant will grow green.

---

135. Sweet, *God's Hotel: A Doctor, a Hospital, and a Pilgrimage to the Heart of Medicine*.

The result?

It was quite amazing how fast Hildegard's prescription worked.

    Within a few weeks I began to see signs of healing deep within Terry's wound. There was no infection, and deep down, at the base of the wound—was it my imagination?—there was a smooth and pink glistening, which was starting to cover and protect her spine. . . .

    It took a long time. It took two and a half years. After two and a half years the bedsore had healed.[136]

This episode is well worth reading in its entirety, and it taught Dr. Sweet what *viriditas* is and that it is very real. The "life force" is part of creation, part of God's gift to us. We and all living things share it as part of our natures. When Hildegard wrote so enthusiastically about the green-ness at work in our world, she was describing an ongoing activity she had actually observed and felt in the landscape in which she lived. Couldn't this ongoing activity be the very same that is alluded to in Genesis by the metaphor of the Tree of Life? In chapter three, I wrote, "The Tree of Life seems to be extreme shorthand for the source of life itself. It is a prescientific concept, explaining the presence of life everywhere in the known world." By using the term *viriditas,* Hildegard was drawing attention to this very quality, one that has seemingly energized the earth from the beginning. The remarkable account of Terry's healing is the kind of connection to real life that the modern sensibility craves. If more such stories can be accumulated, interest in reviving the ancient concepts like the Tree of Life would, I believe, grow exponentially.

The Greening Finger of God

One of the pleasant surprises of this project has been to discover Hildegard to be in fact a way station from ancient times to our own day, a person who transmits the spirit of an earlier era. The high point of

---

136. Sweet, *God's Hotel*, 87–97.

ancient Living Tree conceptions, one could argue, was around 600 CE, the era of Sophronius, whose poetry we read in chapter one. Sophronius and others alive at that time benefited from a sophisticated tradition of interpretation and creativity that was already three centuries old. But 600 CE is fourteen centuries in the past, a very long time ago. Without some signposts and heirs in the interim, the tradition would be quite lost to Western Christians. Hildegard lived more or less in the middle of those fourteen centuries. The resurgence of interest in her spirituality in recent decades has made her into a living force once again. If she is in fact a kind of bearer of an earlier tradition, we moderns who admire her can legitimately feel continuity with the ancient world through an appreciation of her work.

As it happens, we can indeed identify a bridge running from Late Antiquity to the high Middle Ages and Hildegard herself. That bridge is the founder of the monastery at which Hildegard was trained and where she was formed as a religious: a wandering Irish bishop named Disibod. The Rhineland monastery named for him was and is called Disibodberg—the mountain of Disibod. He lived and preached there around 640 CE, some seven centuries before Hildegard came there as a young girl. However, Disibod was not an isolated example of his characteristic spirituality. Disibod was a representative of an entire cadre of wandering evangelists from the Anglo-Irish world who carried Christianity to a still-pagan Northern Europe. These evangelists, of whom Boniface of Mainz is the best known, came from the British Isles to the mainland. They left evidence of their travels as far east as the Balkans. Among the evidence they left were a number of works of art, and the iconography of that art included—what else?—depictions of Paradise and the Tree of Life. In short, the founder of Hildegard's monastery—a man with whom she felt spiritual kinship, as we shall see—was in all probability himself steeped in the Living Tree and Paradise-based living.

The reason we can make such claims about the message of evangelists like Disibod is the art they left behind. Some eighty-five objects in the so-called "Tassilo" style have been catalogued. In an article about the

Tassilo-style objects, which were carried by Anglo-Irish evangelists all across Europe, art historian Egon Wamers comments:

> The Northumbrian design from which the motifs of the Tassilo chalice style are derived was the so-called inhabited vine-scroll, which was introduced into Northumbria at the end of the 7th century as a reflex of the Mediterranean mission. One of its finest manifestations is on the Ormside bowl: the motif of the animals of Creation within the fruit-bearing Tree of Life . . . is the old Mediterranean allegory for eternal life and Paradise. . . . *The promise of salvation and Paradise was the central message of the Christian church for the pagan peoples.* So the Irish monks and the Anglo-Saxon missionaries brought this iconography of Paradise to the barbarian people of the Continent, where it was used to decorate liturgical objects and other, secular, equipment.[137]

As we have seen, one of these wandering evangelists was the Irish bishop Disibod. Around 640 CE he taught and preached in what is now Germany, near the Rhine. After his death the monastery that bears his name was founded, and some centuries later Hildegard of Bingen wrote a song to honor him. Her song, still extant, is "O Viriditas digitas Dei," or as Barbara Newman translates, "O Green Finger of God." It celebrates the Holy Spirit working through Disibod.[138] In fruitful synergy with God's own energies, he brought spiritual vitality to the Rhineland, implies Hildegard, and she compares his spiritual progeny to an orchard that he had planted. Disibod was a kind of Johnny Appleseed of the Spirit! His vivifying gift seemingly endured through centuries, so that the Paradise-based evangelism he exemplified reemerged in Hildegard's amazing ministry.

Accounts of Hildegard herself make one suspect she was more respected than loved. A strong-minded and demanding religious figure, and an aristocrat to boot, she was not exactly the peace-loving hippie that

137. Wamers, "Insular Art in Carolingian Europe," 38, emphasis added.
138. Saint Hildegard of Bingen, *Symphonia: A Critical Edition of the "Symphonia Armonie Celestium Revelationum,"* trans. Newman, 183, 291.

some have imagined. She was traditional in her social views, defending her decision to allow only girls from noble families to enter her convent on the grounds that to admit poor girls would be like mixing different kinds of beasts in the same stall. She was also traditional in ecclesiology, approving of a male-only priesthood. Her spiritual type was not affective but prophetic: "With Hildegard, one does not feel; one sees," comments Caroline Walker Bynum.[139] But what visions she gives us to see! The carefully wrought images of books such as her *Scito Vias Domini (Know the Ways of the Lord)* are not merely the fruits of a creative imagination. They seem clearly to be what she claimed they were: things that she saw—albeit magnificently complex and original.

The notable aspects of her personality are legion. With wonderful spirit she used writing as a tool in an age in which few women were literate at all. Hildegard was full of compassion for the human condition, earnestly seeking the well-being of humanity within the created order as well as the divine. Her concern for healing led to a thoroughly practical knowledge of medicinal herbs. Her waking visions allowed her to look down on creation from above, surrounded with living light.

Something in Hildegard's experience opened her to what interests us here: a sense of the green livingness of things. For this green livingness of things she employed the word *viriditas*. She did not coin the term, but probably found it in the writings of Gregory the Great. Literally "the color green," *viriditas* is a complex concept that Jeanette Jones describes as follows.

> In each case of Gregory and Hildegard, the word *viriditas* has a meaning with respect to a Christian's spiritual life that goes beyond mere references to life, fecundity, or freshness. *Viriditas* implies a particular understanding of the nature of creation and the sovereignty of God. Both authors saw a fallen creation in need of God's redemptive action to save both the earth and themselves, and they both saw this work able to be done only by God Himself. . . . The

---

139. Quoted in Hart and Bishop, *Hildegard of Bingen: Scivias*, 5.

time before Christ's coming is the desolate land or wilderness as the Christian lives in exile from God—a time of lack of *viriditas.* In order to regain a relationship with God, Christ must come and his work on the cross restores that relationship. So that the life of the Christian after Christ is one thriving and flourishing. *Viriditas* is a complex term that encompasses this redemptive background and a continued growing and prospering through a relationship with God.[140]

Certainly the Rhineland region in which she lived is radiant with the green-ness of growing things. A mysterious interplay of heaven and earth in creating life's energies is easy to imagine in such a setting. We have already noted Hildegard's conviction that a human being could be the "greening finger of God." Disibod earned this title in her estimation because of his itinerant evangelism, fruitfully bearing monastic communities such as her own into existence. In an essay about Hildegard as a religious thinker, Professor Constant Mews remarks, "Hildegard develops her thought from organic concepts like 'life' and 'greenness' or 'viridity' *(viriditas).*" This is by contrast with other medieval theologians such as Anselm who "takes for granted the capacity of reason to come to terms with static philosophical concepts like 'being,' 'substance,' and 'accident.'" Yet although Hildegard and thinkers like Anselm differ in their starting place, their foundational insights, they "share a desire to present Christian teaching on the basis of self-evident truths rather than on any imposed authoritative text." Hildegard's visions and her deep innate sensitivity to the beauty of creation convinced her of the self-evident value of life itself as a standard to guide moral and spiritual praxis. For Hildegard, Mews remarks, "the unifying thread is the notion of life itself."[141]

When we seek to be clear about the meaning and action of something so mysterious as the Tree of Life, Hildegard's invented term comes as a gracious gift. *Viriditas* is both precise and evocative, perfect for coming

---

140. Jeanette Jones, "A Theological Interpretation of *Viriditas* in Hildegard of Bingen and Gregory the Great," Portfolio of the Department of Musicology and Ethnomusicology at Boston University 1 (2012): http://www.bu.edu/pdme/jeannette-jones/.
141. Mews, "Religious Thinker," 56–57.

to terms with its real-life meanings. A created energy of ever-new fresh-ness seems to have been in her mind, as well as in the mind of the author of Genesis. Both saw a this-world intermediary between the heavenly fiat of God and the stony inertness of the soil.

Viriditas in Everyday Life

So how can we experience *viriditas* in our own lives? By way of an answer, I propose we consider Hildegard's example more concretely. As an abbess she felt responsible to inculcate her ideas in practical ways. She developed methods to educate the communities over which she had responsibility. She conscientiously shaped the life of the nuns in her care, and the community as a whole. She took this responsibility very seri-ously. Hildegard developed and oversaw daily activities for them and led her charges to further her overall vision of the Christian life. As we have seen, this vision depended heavily on concepts such as *viriditas,* the Spirit-infused greening power that she discerned in creation. Thus her writings and example provide an ideal model for any individual, or for that matter any community, that wishes to take the Tree of Life seriously, and to be nourished by its fruit.

Building upon the self-evident importance of green-ness and grow-ing-ness as signs of the work of the Holy Spirit, Hildegard continuously experimented with ways to let the divine life—what she called "the liv-ing light"—come to fruition in her community. If we approach the vari-ous aspects of her interests as experiments in Christian fruitfulness, we can develop a kind of template of activities for Paradise-based living. To Hildegard, "Paradise still exists as a physical place, 'blooming with the freshness (*viriditas*) of flowers and grass and the charms of spices, full of fine odors.'"[142] Let us then step boldly into this still-existing Paradise with the abbess of Bingen as our guide.

To begin our wanderings in Eden, I propose we focus on three activities Hildegard practiced herself or at any rate inculcated in her

---

142. Ibid., 56.

community: singing, gardening, and creating. They all open vistas on Paradise. Even mere dabbling in them can give a living experience of *viriditas.* We will review her teaching and example in regard to music, the cultivation of herbs, and artistic expression. We then conclude with a reflection on what appears to be the overarching meaning of lived Paradise: the joy of Christian community.

A critical incident in Hildegard's life reveals how highly she regarded the role of music. In the year 1178, the community of which she was abbess was placed under an interdict. (She had given permission to bury an excommunicated nobleman, and the clergy of Mainz cathedral objected.) The interdict suppressed the eucharistic life of the community, and even more poignantly, forbade music in the liturgy. Not being allowed to sing seems to have pained her even more deeply than being deprived of the sacrament. Mews writes:

> Hildegard responded with a letter in which she crystalizes a number of the central features of her thought. . . . She explains that it is through music that humanity can return to the pristine condition of Adam, whose voice originally proclaimed "the sound of every harmony and the sweetness of the whole art of music." Paradise for Hildegard is a place filled with music. Prophets and wise men in the past had devised every kind of melody to express the delight in their soul. This music frightens away the devil. The Psalms of David, when set to music, allow humanity to anticipate the vision of the blessed, when paradise will be restored.[143]

In short, comments Barbara Newman, by depriving her community of song, the clergy "were doing the devil's work and depriving God of his just praise, for which they would in turn be deprived of his company in heaven."[144]

---

143. Ibid., 68.
144. Newman, "'Sibyl of the Rhine': Hildegard's Life and Times," 28. After an intervention by the archbishop of Cologne, the interdict was lifted a few months before Hildegard's death.

This centrality of music to the Christian life was no empty metaphor to Hildegard. She herself wrote liturgical texts and set them to melodies of her own devising. Her compositions are of a unique stamp—as indeed was everything she undertook. What makes them particularly notable was what she attempted to accomplish with them.

> Hildegard's melodies communicate the image not so much of an eternal peace in the next world as of that "fiery life" she sees at the heart of creation. It is through music that her sense of longing for the union of body and soul finds its fullest expression.[145]

Hildegard's music is notable for both its abundance and its florid quality. "Her great responsories are long and ornate," writes Margot Fassler. Their extensive melismas—musical phrases sung on a single vowel—"exceeding by far the norms even of later medieval office repertories."[146] The reasons Hildegard gave for this were theological in nature: "And so the words symbolize the body, and the jubilant music indicates the spirit; and the celestial harmony shows the Divinity, and the words the Humanity of the Son of God."[147] Fassler comments, "Jubilation was frequently expressed in the medieval liturgy by an abundance of notes on a single syllable."[148]

If Hildegard's compositions are innately appealing, they can also seem strange. Not only are they distant in time and style, but their very purpose is unfamiliar. Her music was itself a form of intimacy with God, the dazzling presence of the living Spirit in song. Perhaps an analogy would be the experience of speaking in tongues, in which strange speech is actually a form of prayer.

Most of us understand innately the remarkable power of music. Hildegard puts it in a theological context, but entirely apart from this the gift of music is widely appreciated, and indeed has become a subject

---

145. Mews, "Religious Thinker," 68.
146. Fassler, "Composer and Dramatist," 154.
147. Hart and Bishop, *Hildegard of Bingen: Scivias*, 533.
148. Fassler, "Composer and Dramatist," 154.

of scientific inquiry. Music is known to not only frighten away the devil, but also more prosaically to fight depression. It has many other virtues. Those fortunate enough to belong to active singing groups or other musical ensembles find their participation to be truly life-giving, and they miss it terribly when they are deprived of it, as the nuns of Bingen were for a time.

All of this means that anyone in quest of ways to experience the Tree of Life in daily living can turn with confidence to music as a vehicle. In response to the question, here we are in the New Creation, what now? bursting into song is a tried and true answer. It is not enough to study early art or even to read through interesting liturgies. The New Creation can only come alive when it is lived. In whatever ways we can find to participate actively in music, *viriditas* will flow unhindered.

In the New Creation we might also take a leaf (so to speak) from Eve and Adam, whose primary task was tending God's garden. As explained in chapter one, the *gan* of Eden was not wild, like a National Park. It was a space cultivated by human labor and ingenuity, like the Hanging Gardens of Babylon. Hikers can walk through a beautiful forest and (ideally) leave no trace of their passage, but a gardener interacting with the natural order changes the landscape. Gardening requires hands-on effort. Eve and Adam must have gotten dirt under their nails and grass stains (pure *viriditas*) on their knees. The flourishing of nature under the guidance of human creativity is, like music, a phenomenon that Hildegard saw as deeply congruent with God's original purposes for humanity.

Hildegard wrote movingly about the beauty of trees and flowers as symbols of God's love. However, she had a special concern for the cultivation of plants with medicinal value. The leaves of the Tree of Life are for healing, so it is appropriate that medieval monasteries practiced the healing arts. As abbess, she oversaw an infirmary for the care of the sick and a garden for growing of medicinal herbs. She also wrote extensively about medical matters. In an article on Hildegard as a medical writer, Florence Eliza Glaze describes both her originality and also ways she was typical of her age.

She was, as a medical thinker, clearly interested in the broader universal context through which she might understand and explain the reasons for diseases, both cosmic and microcosmic, as well as revealing the means by which diseases might be vanquished.[149]

Within this context the power of humans to know and use created things is

> a knowledge granted by God . . . deserving special attention. Thus "the good and useful herbs," and the "bad and useless ones" . . . can only be known through informed discernment, part of the knowledge of the powers or "virtues" of created things which God had granted to Adam at his creation.[150]

We do not possess details of her actual involvement in the healing work of her convent, but we do have her book, *Physica,* which catalogs the medicinal qualities and uses of plants and many other elements.[151] Whether Hildegard herself spent much time in the garden is unknowable. But what is certain is that she valued the knowledge and the work of gardening. It is difficult to see how she could have developed such a thorough appreciation of *viriditas* without at least a little time actually cultivating plants.

For a more modern version of this approach to gardening, the interested reader might look into a volume appropriately entitled *Back to Eden.* Written in the 1930s by a minister and wandering evangelist for natural healing named Jethro Kloss, this rambling but charming text has become a classic of the contemporary natural healing movement. It includes over six hundred pages of descriptions of illnesses and the natural remedy appropriate to each, often citing Scripture and God's plans for humanity. Kloss also uses language reminiscent of Hildegard to frame his subject:

---

149. Glaze, "Medical Writer," 133.
150. Ibid., 137.
151. Ibid., 132.

When God had created this world and made a beautiful garden, he put the tree of life in it, the leaves of which were for the healing of the nations. The Lord told them to eat freely of this tree, because that tree was especially designed to keep them well. This tree corresponds with the tree of life that is found in the Paradise of God, of which the redeemed are going to eat freely. When man was driven from the Garden of Eden and had no more access to the tree of life, God added herbs to man's diet and God expects that we shall partake of them to keep us from getting sick. They are one of God's remedial agencies for afflicted humanity and his plan was that everyone should raise herbs in his garden and gather those that grow wild everywhere and use them, when needed.[152]

The nuns of Rupertsberg would have felt at home with this book. The great popularity of natural remedies, and the continuing interest of many in knowing and growing herbs, shows the affinity we still have with this vision of Edenic medicine.

However, those who love gardening will need no mere book to persuade them that it is a restorative and health-giving activity. They readily call it addictive, by which they mean not that it is harmful, but that when practiced frequently, it leaves one wanting more. Patient waiting for a plant to emerge into its full beauty, and the excitement of coming out one morning and finding it so, is thrilling. Well does this author remember the amazement of seeing the first flower he ever planted—a marigold—suddenly in bloom. The natural world is indeed a miracle, and *viriditas*, although of the natural order, is also of the Spirit. Thus in whatever way we have of cultivating the earth, and nurturing plants both practical and merely beautiful, we will be in touch with the New Creation.

A third way Hildegard models the direct experience of a New Creation is the path of artistic creativity. The amount of time and energy she expended in artistic endeavor is most impressive. Creative work was

---

152. Kloss, *Back to Eden*, 169.

for her not time wasted. Making new beauty and finding vehicles for fresh meaning were to her as deeply human as anything else we devote ourselves to, and worthy of the greatest care.

Hildegard's massive musical output has already been mentioned: "She is quite simply the most prolific composer of monophonic chants known to us, not only from the twelfth century but from the entire Middle Ages."[153] However, we have so far only alluded in passing to her creativity in the visual arts, which was equally remarkable. Her *Scivias*, or Book of Divine Knowledge, is replete with fascinating images that she personally devised to accompany her texts. Although it is uncertain to what extent she was an illustrator in her own right, it seems probable that she gave specific instructions to trained artisans who did the actual illuminations.[154]

It is also highly probable that the designs she created had been revealed to her in visionary experiences. Some aspects of her art suggest optical effects associated with migraines, to which she was apparently susceptible.[155] These factors also indicate that Hildegard was not perhaps herself a typical practitioner of the visual arts. However, that illustrations should complement the message of her texts clearly mattered to her. She worked diligently to perfect them over many years. Her artistic work may have been at second hand, but surely she took the satisfaction in seeing her visions take form on paper, made incarnate to the eye of beholders. Caviness concludes:

> The distinction between making art and having it made was less clear in the Middle Ages than it is now. I believe that Hildegard can be credited with the quintessential part of creativity that Renaissance theorists regarded as the highest level of artistic creativity, that is, *idea* or concept.[156]

---

153. Fassler, "Composer and Dramatist," 150.
154. Caviness, "Artist," 112.
155. Ibid., 113.
156. Ibid., 124.

Finally, there is her prodigious output of poetry to be considered. Most of her poetry was written to be sung. Her texts are indivisible from the music that she created for them, and from their living role in the liturgical life of her community. Nevertheless, read simply as poetry, the texts are remarkable as well, and repay careful study. Her formal training in Latin and in the conventions of literature was perhaps more rough and ready than that of male counterparts. Nevertheless, her imagery is striking and her verse is energetic, colorful, and thought-provoking. Barbara J. Newman's fascinating translations of her verse into a more modern style bring them alive for those who may not read Latin themselves. They are a labor of love, in the spirit of the great original, the abbess of Bingen.[157]

All in all, anyone who wishes to follow Hildegard's example would do well to give time and space to the creative impulse. Busy modern people tend to think that only activities having economic value are worth their attention. But this is short-sighted. Whether it is song or poetry or the fine arts, or other arenas entirely which human ingenuity has devised—woodworking or cooking or interior decorating to name but a few, cocreation with God is a role Hildegard would insist we were created to fulfill. What to do in the New Creation? Make something new, of beauty and of import.

I am pleased to share some imagery of contemporary persons who have been inspired by the Tree of Life theme and used their creative gifts to make art. They are innately charming, and the makers report that the process of creation was as important to them as the resulting art itself.

A Yet More Excellent Way

Singing, gardening, creating—all are excellent ways to pass one's time in Paradise. Each activity fulfills some aspect of our created nature, and gives access to the flow of *viriditas* around and through us. However, it may be doubted whether a life totally dedicated even to these excellent

---

157. Saint Hildegard of Bingen, *Symphonia*.

activities would, in the end, by themselves alone constitute a full restoration of Edenic existence. If Christ's work is to reopen Paradise, there is more to it.

In chapter three, while considering the biblical account of the Garden, I observed, "In the first Paradise, humans at first enjoyed intimacy with God, with creation, and with one another. Indeed, intimacy on all these levels is a good working definition of what Paradise really could mean."

On this understanding, the Fall would consist of separation and alienation within and among each of these arenas. (We do indeed see a good deal of such alienation in our world!) Restoration then could only mean a reestablishment of the original community which the first humans enjoyed on each of these levels, and especially, I would argue, among our fellow humans. This theme allows one last look back to Hildegard, who lived her entire life in community. As a vowed religious living under the Benedictine rule, her manner of life differed from that of most practicing Christians. Nevertheless, the care and exertions she undertook to found and mold communities as abbess shows clearly the

A Tree of Life theme for the Cross created by Mandy Black at a women's retreat. (Credit: Rev. Judith Kessler, used by permission.)

A banner by artist Sally Herring graces the chapel at the Duncan Gray Retreat Center in Mississippi. The Tree/Cross surmounting a globe reminds one of the Armenian khach-kar design. (Credit: Aileen Loranger, used by permission.)

importance she ascribed to life together. Intriguingly, the clearest statement of how she understood her own role may be found not in what she wrote of herself, but about—who else?—Disibod. Her *vita* about the saint "may be read for its amazing parallels to her experience," according to John Van Engen.

> The saint, she narrates, gathered "a congregation of fifty perfect brothers in only twelve years." . . . He converted their hearts to the teachings of Benedict. . . . He gathered devoted followers who understood that the life was to be "hard warfare against the self," rejecting people who engaged in religious life only for show in favor of those who sought "the sweet consolation of a quieted mind."[158]

---

158. Van Engen, *Abbess*, 41.

It does indeed sound as though Hildegard is writing about herself, mod-
estly (and shrewdly) hiding herself beneath the model of Disibod.

> [Hildegard] did not think of her house as a residence for ladies
> but as a school for virtue. . . . She often adopted the image of a gar-
> dener, with the abbess as the gardener and the flowers or herbs cul-
> tivated into full bloom as the virtues alive in her subjects. The goal
> towards which a person was to strive, in herself or in her charges,
> was "greenness" and "fragrance."[159]

As a good Benedictine, she believed that all this schooling of souls could
most fruitfully be accomplished in a communal setting, believers working together in intimate mutual care.

The inference to be drawn is that our own communities of worship
and service are a critical venue for experiencing New Creation. A congregation should be more than just an agglomeration of people; it should
be a little Paradise of mutual affection and common service. When I

*Images of Christ sprout from the
branches of a tree in this collage created by Hope Lennartz.* (Credit: Hope
Lennartz, used by permission.)

159. Ibid., 48.

make this point, I sometimes ask people whether their particular congregation is in fact a little Paradise. Almost always the answer comes in the form of chuckles and wry laughter: "Not really" would be a common answer. But this invites the questions: Why not? What is blocking the free flow of *viriditas* among the members? As Victoria Sweet realized in the case of Terry, Hildegard would first ask herself what was blocking the free flow in her patient.

> What she would do, I suddenly saw, was remove obstructions to Terry's *viriditas*, to Terry's natural ability to heal. Because if nothing was in the way, then *viriditas* would heal her wound as surely as a plant will grow green.[160]

Might we not suspect that in the same way, the free movement of the Holy Spirit in a congregation should almost automatically bring spiritual vitality? Thus the presence or absence of *viriditas* in a Christian community could be a useful diagnostic for leaders to undertake as they assess its well-being.

When the Spirit is flowing freely, and a Christian community really does function as it is intended to do, it can indeed be a joyful and life-giving experience for all. There are many examples, and even people who chuckle and smile wryly about their own parish will acknowledge that they have felt this joy at least on certain occasions. The mutual support in times of adversity, the great happiness of transformative worship, the sense of accomplishment when outreach or social justice have been addressed, and even the holy gossip of a covered-dish supper are what keep the members coming back for more. The greenness and fragrance of such settings can become quite addictive.

Two Objections

Now would be a good time to mention some objections to the forgoing ideas that I have encountered and would like to address. They came at

---

160. Sweet, *God's Hotel*, 95.

a conference where a preliminary version of the Life-Giving Tree idea was presented, alongside the ideas of singing, gardening, and creating as vehicles for Paradise-based living. There were two interconnected objections.

The first objection is that the real world in which we actually live is anything but a Paradise: there is injustice, war, gun violence, racism, sexism. The Church is called to stand in witness against these things, and for practices that cultivate mutual respect and love. To withdraw into gardening and hymn singing would be to abdicate our responsibility to address evils and advocate for social justice. Second, there are many people whose lives are so burdened by the struggles of daily life that they do not have time or energy to sing, garden, and paint. Those highbrow activities were all well and good for Hildegard and her patrician followers, but not for many of today's poor whom Jesus especially loves.

Let me say that these are very fair objections. I have thought about them a good deal, and have changed some of my lines of argument in response. So, for example, I have realized that "Paradise" is too vague and loaded a term for much of what I want to convey, and have begun using "New Creation" more frequently instead. "New Creation" is better anchored in the New Testament than is "Paradise," and so is a more precise and less freighted expression.

However, in more direct response to the objections, I would say first of all that a common quest for social justice is exactly the kind of activity that people who are made new in Christ should undertake. The New Creation and its Church exist so that the whole world can be transformed. People who worship together and then advocate together are "in Christ," so the intimacy of the new order is available for those who work together for a better world. The struggle for justice can be alarming and dangerous. However, it also engenders closeness and solidarity, both of which are aspects of the New Creation. Those who work together under trying circumstances can still feel the power of life moving among them. The civil rights marchers of the 1960s sang as they walked, and remember to this day the feelings of mutual support and the pride they took in what they accomplished, in spite of the resistance they encountered. In short, an assertive call for social justice is precisely the sort of fruit of the spirit that one would expect from a Christian community that is alive in the Spirit. Hildegard, so far as we know, did not march with placards in her day, but today she might well do so. What is to prevent her from being one of the "nuns on a bus"? And if she wrote a song about the experience, all the better. Strong advocates for a better world can certainly experience their activism as a movement of *viriditas* in the real world, and as proof of the reality of a New Creation in Christ. Thus I believe Living Tree imagery is not incompatible with an assertive stand for social justice; in fact, it can be a source of strength amid the struggle.

As for persons too burdened to sing or garden, I would simply say that my recent experience of living in Haiti for nearly a year has been instructive. Haiti is, as everyone knows and one gets tired of hearing, the poorest nation in the Western hemisphere. If life is difficult anywhere, it is difficult there. People fortunate enough to have a way of making some money rise early and work hard all day. Yet I have never been in a society that values creativity more highly, or is more likely to burst into song. A vibrant culture of the arts exists in Haiti, as the Tree of Life image on the facing page demonstrates.

The omnipresent minibuses called "tap-taps" are a colorful riot of popular design: pictures of birds, of saints, of soccer players, and just bright colors are visible everywhere one goes. Average people know songs by heart and are apt to break out singing them at virtually any moment, and start dancing to boot. The workday may be long, but is accompanied by signs of liveliness and vitality that compare favorably to those in wealthier lands. Gardening is everywhere—by necessity in a land that is so rural in its economy. A love of growing things is present, as the stacks of fresh fruit at every market will testify. In short, the very ingredients that Hildegard identified as sources of *viriditas* for her nuns are life-sustaining activities also among the poorest of the poor in today's Haiti. One shudders to think what Haiti would be without them:

a land with no hope at all. With them, Haiti is a nation that, in spite of its challenges, regularly evokes admiration from those who take the trouble to get to know it. So there really does not need to be a disjunction between poverty and the ways of cultivating *viriditas* we have taken from Hildegard. They can give life in many situations, including ones we might not at first suspect.

Still, I appreciate the objections. It is always good to be kept honest. The risk one runs in reviving an ancient idea is that archaic social principles can come along for the ride. The social worlds of Sophronius and of Hildegard are not ones we would choose to live in, and so their ideas need to be updated for modern times. How to do this is itself a creative quest that calls for spiritual vitality and lively minds, and that would be life-giving to venture upon.

Going Deeper

- Do you believe that *viriditas* really exists?
- To what do you attribute the healing of Terry Becker?
- Are singing, gardening, or creating part of your life? If so, are they in fact effective ways to get in touch with nature's power of

Metal saved from oil drums is often creatively recycled by Haitian artists, as is the case with this lively image of a Paradise-like setting made by an unknown contemporary artisan. The birds in the tree reminds one of the Ethiopian cast bronze cross discussed in chapter two, and the early Coptic carving as well. (Credit: author.)

continuous re-creation, symbolized by the Tree of Life? If not, what other ways do you know to experience *viriditas*?

- Is your congregation "a little Paradise"? If not, why not? If so, why exactly do you think so?
- If Hildegard were alive today, how would she address economic inequality? Terrorism? Climate change?

6

Fruits of the Tree of Life

There is hope for a tree,
if it is cut down, that it will sprout again,
and that its shoots will not cease.
Though its root grows old in the earth,
and its stump dies in the ground,
yet at the scent of water it will bud
and put forth branches like a young plant.
                              —Job 14:7–9

Scripture says that after they ate from the Tree of the Knowledge of Good and Evil our first parents were banished from Eden. This was to prevent humanity (whom Adam and Eve represent) from also eating the fruit of the other tree in the midst of the Garden, the Tree of Life. Eating from this tree would have made them immortal. God did not want that to happen. Looking honestly at the course of human history and what harm our species has caused with even just our limited lifespans, it is hard to disagree with the wisdom of heaven. In any event, to forestall attempts on our part to return to Eden, cherubim were positioned at its eastern gates, wielding fiery swords (Gen. 3:22–24).

This state of exile from life continued until the time of Jesus, who reversed it in a remarkable act of divine acceptance. Jesus gave us the

Eucharist to be, at long last, the food that confers immortality: "Whoever eats of this bread will live for ever," he said (John 6:51). We may therefore plausibly see the Eucharist as the new fruit of the Tree of Life, which (as we have been saying at length) may easily be identified with the Cross. Art forms such as the vine-scrolls of Anglo-Saxon crosses and Armenian khachkars make just such an identification. Their abundant clusters of grapes symbolize the wine of the cup of salvation, and thus proclaim the Eucharist to be fruit borne by the Life-Giving Cross. Those who enjoy poetic thinking will find this a lovely image, as effective a sign of human immortality as the story of exile from Eden had been of our mortality. Those who think more literally will find the promise of life everlasting—conveyed by the consecrated bread—personally helpful to them amid their travails.

However, the New Testament does not limit the concept of spiritual fruit to the Holy Eucharist. Paul uses the metaphor of fruit to expound the spiritual life itself. He speaks of fruit of the Spirit: "love, joy, peace, patience, kindness, generosity, faithfulness, gentleness, and self-control" (Gal. 5:22–23). Notably, he relates his insight about these inspiring qualities to the work of the Cross for, after listing them, he almost immediately adds, "And those who belong to Christ Jesus have crucified the flesh with its passions and desires" (Gal. 5:24). I would argue this gives us warrant to also consider the Cross as the Tree that bears the fruits of the Spirit. Indeed the metaphor of fruit works well together with the metaphor of a tree: fruit is borne by a slow process of ripening on a branch, and branches grow on trees, so the association is natural. Viewing the Cross as the channel of spiritual fruitfulness makes a world of sense.

So far we have been discussing the spiritual meaning of the Cross for individual piety. This chapter will argue that the concept of the Cross as Life-Giving Tree also has the welcome power of bringing peace to conflicted situations involving groups. Unfortunately, however, we must first confront the fact that the Cross has itself been at the heart of many conflicted situations. We will review three of them in quest of ways in which viewing the Cross as a Life-Giving Tree may bear fruit such as kindness, gentleness, and patience amid those struggles.

Conflicts of the Cross

In a blog entry entitled "Christianity Divided by the Cross," posted on *Patheos* on October 25, 2013, theologian Marcus Borg observed that "American Christians are deeply divided by the cross of Jesus—namely, by how they see the meanings of his death." He described this division as follows:

> At the risk of labels and broad generalizations, "conservative" Christians generally believe a "payment" understanding of the cross: Jesus died to pay for our sins so we can be forgiven.
>
> [On the other hand,] most "progressive" Christians (at least a majority) have great difficulty with the "payment" understanding. Many reject it. Some insist that rather than focusing on Jesus's death, we should instead focus on his life and teachings.[161]

Thus Borg waded fearlessly into contemporary conflicts over the theological concept of the Atonement, the mechanism whereby Jesus restored us to intimacy with God. To atone is to be "at-one," and articulating the exact manner in which this occurs is indeed a source of controversy. I do not wish to take part in this controversy in this chapter. Like so many conversations of a theological nature, this one sometimes gives the impression that the champions on either side are not really listening to one another, and are locked in to their positions on a deep, heartfelt level. To attempt to evaluate their positions, even with the best will in the world, runs the risk of being seen as being merely another exponent of one of these well-defined positions, and, once again, not really being heard. To his credit, Borg makes his own position clear. Speaking of partisans of the "progressive" point of view, he says, "They are right about what they affirm." He proceeds to a critique of the "conservative" point

---

161. Marcus Borg, "Christianity Divided by the Cross," *Patheos,* October 25, 2013, www.patheos.com/blogs/marcusborg/2013/10/christianity-divided-by-the-cross/.

of view, although generously soliciting comments and conversation from all comers, and even admonishing "progressives" that by de-emphasizing the Cross they "risk impoverishing the meaning of Jesus."[162]

Without taking sides in the debate, we can nevertheless affirm that Borg is correct in calling attention to it. He also is effective in laying out its terms and of saying that how we conceptualize the Cross of Jesus is at the heart of the question. Thus, even though he is a protagonist in the controversy, we can usefully employ his analysis to get a sense of the issues at play.

Borg first articulates the "payment for sins" model favored by conservatives. He states this model received its classical articulation in 1098 by the theologian Anselm in his work with the Latin title *Cur Deus Homo?* which means "Why Did God Become Human?" Borg says, "Anselm's purpose was to provide a rational argument for the necessity of the incarnation and death of Jesus." He did this by appropriating a cultural model of the Middle Ages, in which the honor of a feudal Lord was an important social factor.

> Anselm then applied that model to our relationship with God. We have been disobedient and deserve to be punished. And yet God loves us and wants to forgive us. But the price of sin must be paid. Jesus as a human being who was also divine and thus perfect and without sin did that.[163]

This way of explaining Christ's work is known as "substitutionary atonement."

In a subsequent post, after receiving comments, Borg drew on another classic text to help argue the weaknesses of the substitutionary atonement model.[164] *Christus Victor* was written in 1931 by Swedish scholar Gustav Aulén. Borg says, "I read Aulén's book almost fifty years

---

162. Ibid.

163. Ibid.

164. Marcus Borg, "Further Comments about the Cross: Part Three," *Patheos,* October 31, 2013, http://www.patheos.com/blogs/marcusborg/2013/10/further-comments-about-the -cross-part-three/.

ago. His argument was persuasive then, and in the decades since has become even more so." In brief, Aulén argued that in the first millennium typical accounts of atonement stressed Christ's victory over sin, death, and the devil. Rather than paying a debt, Christ triumphed over humanity's great foes, and made us beneficiaries of his victory. This is the model that Aulén preferred, and he further argued that Luther's theology was an attempt to restore it.

As a progressive, Borg approves of Aulén's analysis, but wants to augment and update it. Borg would add that Christ's victory should be seen as operative also in systems of political domination. Borg wants to emphasize "the historical and political causes of Jesus's death: 'the powers' who killed him were the political and religious powers of his time." He notes that "the earliest and New Testament understandings of [the Cross are] that it reveals the moral bankruptcy of 'the powers,' the domination system that executed Jesus; and that death and resurrection are an archetype, an incarnation of the way, the path, of personal transformation."[165]

The comment about personal transformation also connects to the third type of atonement theology identified by Aulén, a more modern approach that he called the "moral exemplar" theory. Borg summarizes this model by saying that it teaches "Jesus's death provides us with a moral example that we should follow." Aulén found this to be a weak and inadequate response to an over-rigid reliance on substitutionary atonement. Borg finds more to be said for it. Borg writes:

> I think that [Aulén] dismisses the third too cavalierly and that his name for it is unfortunate. Perhaps for him as a Lutheran, the third understanding sounded too much like "works." But the archetype of "dying and rising with Christ" is not really about "works," something we must do in order to be saved. Rather, it is about the personal transformation at the center of the Christian life. It is not

---

165. Ibid.

about "how to behave" as much as it is about "how to be changed." Behavior will follow.[166]

Thus three short blog posts give a sense of the theological subtleties of the current divisions over the Cross. I would add that these seemingly abstruse subtleties can quickly translate into strongly felt emotional responses. Consider, for example, the diverging reactions to the film *The Passion of the Christ*. This film could be understood as a depiction of substitutionary atonement in a graphic form. By dwelling at length on the physical agonies of Christ, it draws attention to the immense debt he was paying for us. Many persons on the progressive end of the spectrum are viscerally offended by what appears to be its glorification of the wrath of God. On the other hand, conservatives experience the film as a moving tribute to divine self-offering; I know people who watch it each year on Easter Day as a part of their celebration.

Wherever one falls on the spectrum, I think we all can agree that the theological issues have been under discussion for a very long time, and that they really do influence the way one thinks of the Cross. That being the case, we might ask how understanding the Cross as the Life-Giving Tree, opening the way to a new paradise of intimacy with God, with neighbor, and with creation, bears on the divisions Borg articulates. My answer would be that images of the Cross as the Tree of Life seem to be coming from a completely different spiritual mindset. Rather than simply reprising a debate, they offer a refreshing third way. Greater awareness of the tradition of the Life-Giving Tree could well reconcile divergent points of view, or at least create the possibility of the shared experience of the New Creation.

The reason for this hope for peace among warring factions is that the Life-Giving Tree draws our attention to a different point in the narrative than the one at issue. As Borg put it at the outset, what is being debated today is the meaning of Christ's death. But the Life-Giving Tree imagery

---

166. Ibid.

focuses not on his death, but on the fruits of his death, that is, what comes after: the new state in which we find ourselves once death has been overcome. Rather than addressing only Jesus's death and its meaning, the Cross of the Living Tree focuses our attention on the results of Christ's work. Without attempting to unravel the mechanisms of redemption, it simply invites us to join the risen Christ in the New Creation. The Life-Giving Cross does not deny the death of Christ; after all, it is still a symbol of the instrument of his death. But it is transformed just as Christ's crucified body was and revealed for what it was intended to be from the beginning: a gracious symbol of God's unending purpose of giving life. A transfigured Cross invites us to enjoy and develop the fruits of the Tree of Life, such as immortality, love, joy, and peace. In a single bound, it carries us past the finally unknowable puzzle of the mechanisms of redemption to settle in a happy contemplation of its results.

What a happy result it could be if ardent progressives and ardent conservatives, after a day of rousing theological debate about atonement, could somehow let go of their entrenched positions and experience together some of the fruits of the Life-Giving Tree. Perhaps something as simple as sitting together and gazing in silence at the Coptic sanctuary curtain of chapter two would accomplish this. At any rate, the Tree invites such experimentation.

A second kind of conflict occasioned by the Cross is that which arises from misuse of this symbol. Unfortunately, there are many examples of this, which those of us on the inside of Christian communities tend to forget. One terrifying modern example is the burning cross employed by the Ku Klux Klan. Although it seems obvious to most Christians that this is a very twisted and even demonic application, the fact remains that what the KKK employs is indeed a form of the cross. Our beloved symbol can be used to create fear and to intimidate the innocent. Not unlike the burning crosses is the Nazi symbol, the swastika. Again, believers may object that this symbol of a warped regime is not a cross, but this perspective is not universally appreciated. The fact that the Nazi regime arose in a basically Christian environment is sometimes thought to explain the use of a cross-like symbol to represent it.

A third example of misuse shows a family resemblance to the first two: the use of crosses to intimidate the Jews of eastern Europe and Russia prior to World War II. Pogroms led by "Christ-loving" Cossacks are associated in the minds of Jews with the cross as a symbol of oppression to this day. Jewish author Yossi Klein Halevi, for example, speaks of the dread his father experienced. He writes:

> Historically, [Holy Week] was a time of Jewish trauma. In my father's town in Transylvania, Jews would lock themselves in their homes before Easter, hiding from their Christian neighbors, who blamed them personally for the crucifixion. Even for me, growing up in 1960s America, the crucifix had been a threat and a taunt. I would cross the street rather than pass my neighborhood's only church just to avoid the crucifix hanging outside, which seemed to me a celebration of Jewish death.[167]

Halevi later became a journalist in Israel and conceived a desire to pray and worship with Christians and Muslims in the Holy Land. His book *At the Entrance to the Garden of Eden* tells of the many remarkable encounters that ensued. This lovely book is well worth reading by anyone who favors better interfaith understanding. Even in tense modern times, he was able to locate people of faith and integrity who saw the value of experimenting with actual interfaith prayer on more than a superficial level. He prayed with Catholic nuns, Sufi clerics, and Messianic Jews, among others, and learned something from them all.

As part of his quest, Halevi sought to observe holy days with his hosts, going to Bethlehem at Christmas, for instance. Holy Week, however, presented a special difficulty. He found that he was feeling lethargic and unable to find a Christian community to worship with. He writes that he eventually discovered a simple reality: "I was afraid of Holy Week." He discussed this issue with a conservative rabbi, who asked him, "How

167. Halevi, *At the Entrance to the Garden of Eden*, 137.

will you handle all those crosses?" Then the rabbi "took two knives on the table and formed them into a cross. He defined my problem with brutal precision: intimacy with the cross meant betraying all those Jews who'd been killed in its name."[168]

After exploring options for a Christian community with whom to experience Good Friday, Halevi ended by choosing an Armenian church. He made his way to the ancient Armenian quarter in Jerusalem, surrounded by a massive stone wall, which to Halevi symbolized its "wounded isolationism," reflecting the Armenian experience of genocide in the early twentieth century. "Yet it was precisely their trauma," he realized, "that might provide the solution to my Easter dilemma. What better way to outwit a Jew's fear of Christianity than to experience Holy Week with a Christian community that had itself suffered genocide?"[169]

However there was a second reason that the Armenian community turned out to be particularly well chosen in regard to Halevi's quest to understood Holy Week: the form of the cross itself was more accessible. The monk who became his guide pointed out in the monastery's courtyard

> a large stone cross: a *khatchkar,* the ancient Armenian cross of resurrection, whose extremities ended in flowers, resembling a tree in bloom. It was a beautiful cross. And it reminded me of the logo I'd seen of a Holocaust survivor organization: a row of barbed wire sprouting into a bud. Our two peoples shared the same religious impulse to invest suffering with meaning, the same expectation of a redemptive end.
>
> "Armenian churches never display crucifixes," the monk explained. "We see the cross as the symbol of life, not suffering." It was as if some prophetic instinct in the Armenian soul had understood that a people destined for crucifixion would require a cross of comfort.[170]

---

168. Ibid., 138.
169. Ibid., 150.
170. Ibid., 154.

A subsequent conversation with an Armenian layman named George confirmed this intuition. In the conversation, Halevi and George talked about God's seeming absence amid suffering.

> "Do Armenians identify with Jesus' helplessness on the cross?" I asked. "Or do you see it as a symbol for God's silence?"
>
> "You know that our cross isn't a crucifix. Out of a hundred thousand Armenian stone crosses that have been discovered, only three are crucifixes. If we had emphasized the crucifixion, I don't think we would have had the strength to survive. When I see a crucifix, even in a museum as a work of art, I can't look at it. It's unbearable for me."
>
> I explained my fear of the cross and that I'd come to the Armenians on Holy Week because I sensed I would be "safe" among them, that they wouldn't see me as one of the crucifiers but the crucified.
>
> George said, "Menachem Begin once said that when he looks into the eyes of an Armenian, he sees a Jew. When I look into your eyes, I see an Armenian."[171]

There could not be a clearer illustration of how a symbol—a work of religious art—can come to represent the historical experience of an entire people than this narrative of Halevi. Whether as a sign causing dread, as to Jews, or of hope for renewal after unutterable pain, as for Armenians, he demonstrates that the Cross has power. This being so, we can only urge that the peace-making properties of Living Tree images of the Cross come as a real gift. They give us a way of addressing the problems of cross imagery frankly with outsiders, and yet retaining confidence in a symbol that expresses all that is most hopeful in our faith. It is hard to see how the Tree of Life could inspire fear or dread, or how it could be misused. It is a positive sign quite resistant to negative misinterpretation. The Life-Giving Tree cannot threaten death to others; it can only invite one and all to a contemplation of the New Creation that it so readily proclaims.

---

171. Ibid., 164–65.

The third kind of conflict involving the Cross is that which conflates the Cross with Western imperialistic values. At the time of the Crusades, to "take the Cross" meant that a Western Christian adopted the symbol in a militant mode for war against the armies of Islam. The association has lost much of its force in modern Western circles, where a "crusader" now means merely a person who strives single-mindedly for any good cause. The term "crusade" by the same token can be applied to any good cause, ranging to fixing potholes in city streets to significant educational reform. But the original force is still strong in militant Islamic circles, where NATO troops are routinely identified with the crusading knights of the Middle Ages. Today's struggle with Western values is seen as being in continuity with that of centuries ago, and the cross is still the symbol of all that ISIS and Al Qaeda despise. Christians may protest that there is no explicit Christian connection with (for instance) the invasions of Iraq and Afghanistan, but on the symbolic level it is far too late to complain. The cross, like it or not, symbolizes Western secular imperialism in the minds of many.[172]

Another situation in which the cross has been taken to generally symbolize Western imperialism is in China. In recent years Christianity has spread rapidly there, especially in evangelical modes. According to a *New York Times* article dated May 21, 2016, there are now sixty million Christians in China, part of a widespread resurgence in religious values that has also included Buddhism, Taoism, and Islam. A previous policy of religious toleration is under review, and tighter controls are expected across the board. In regard to control of Christianity, this has translated into a pilot project of forced removal of crosses from churches in Zhenjang Province. In that province between 1,200 and 1,700 spires

---

172. A further medieval association has confused Westerners. ISIS spokesmen have promised the destruction of Rome. To secular Westerners, this sounds like a particular and puzzling aversion to Italians, but in fact "Rome" was the name for Constantinople in the wars of the Middle Ages. ISIS is evoking the millennial ambition of Islamic forces to overcome the empire that frustrated them for some many centuries, and finally fell in 1453 CE.

had already been forcibly removed when the article was written. "In a major speech on religious policy," President Xi Jinpeng "urged the ruling Communist Party to 'resolutely guard against overseas infiltrations via religious means,' and he warned that religions in China must 'Sinicize,' or become Chinese."[173] Worship and regular congregational life continue more or less as before, but the outer and visible symbol of Christianity, it would seem, symbolizes non-Chinese values, and therefore must be removed. The article notes that this policy runs a risk in that Christianity has indeed become inculturated in China, becoming popular with educated white-collar workers, for instance. Nevertheless, tying the cross to foreign influence was a plausible strategy for the government to employ, giving us yet another example of how this symbol can be used and misused.

Would the situations described above be in any way different if the cross symbol used by believers were depicted as alive and life-giving? Surely we are in a purely speculative realm with such a question. It seems utterly unlikely that ISIS or Al Qaeda would be impressed by any symbols other than their own, or for that matter interested in irenic initiatives of any sort. The Chinese situation might be somewhat different. For one thing, Christianity first arrived in China by 600 CE, in a Nestorian form. As we have seen, the Nestorian cross is of the leaved-cross type. Thus, a reasonable response to the government's policy of forced cross removal could well include the argument that Christianity does indeed have deep Chinese roots. If these roots could include a form of the cross such as we have seen in India, where its living roots are depicted as a lotus plant, the argument would be even stronger.

In any event the deepest appeal of the Living Cross motif is that it evokes patient vegetative kinds of growth that are inherently universal and deeply pacific. A tree that gives life is, or ought to be, as non-threatening a symbol as one could devise. Thus in a thought experiment,

---

173. Ian Johnson, "Decapitated Churches in China's Christian Heartland," *New York Times*, May 21, 2016, Section A, Page 6.

perhaps the Tree of Life symbolism could flourish more irenically even in today's China. It is not a symbol of only Western values, but of aspirations that are deeply human, shared by all.

Summing It Up

In the introduction I remarked upon the fact "that the theme of a New Creation is deeply rooted in tradition, and so is the symbol of the Cross as a Life-Giving Tree." I also stated that, "I began to wonder: What is Christian life like when it is intentionally organized around that theme and that symbol?" and went on to say that this book would be a thought-experiment in quest of answers to that question. I hope that I have managed to explain what I now think the principle of the New Creation is, and that my suggestions of ways of implementing it in daily life are at least a beginning for those who might want to try intentionally organizing their lives around it and its very attractive symbol, the Life-Giving Tree. Steps as simple as singing more, or gardening more, will help. So will directed efforts to witness effectively in community for social justice, or making the free flow of *viriditas* an explicit benchmark for parish vitality. Other creative minds will no doubt envision further applications of the idea that we are already, by grace, in a condition of renewed intimacy with God, with neighbor, and with creation that one could reasonably (or at any rate optimistically) describe as a reopened paradise.

Even so there is, at least to me, a final question yet remaining. Granted that "a New Creation" is a coherent organizing principle for the Christian life, but it must also be admitted that there are other ways of conceptualizing this life. Why should one prefer "a New Creation," or as I sometimes also like to call it, "the gospel of a renewed Paradise," to those other ways of organizing our faith? Is there evidence that it is fruitful, that it works? The vision of the New Creation is inherently appealing, but I confess that I have also frequently wondered what I could point to as proof of its value. Paul, perhaps in a similar frame of mind, wrote to the Corinthians:

My speech and my proclamation were not with plausible words of wisdom, but with a demonstration of the Spirit and of power, so that your faith might rest not on human wisdom but on the power of God. (1 Cor 2:4–5)

Would that I had similar demonstrations of Spirit and power to bear witness to *viriditas*!

There are indeed hints in what I have experienced personally, beginning with the undoubted fact that almost everyone to whom I have showed the images found in chapter two has been excited and pleased, and wanted to know more. Sustained applause after two different presentations to knowledgeable groups of Christians and sustained interest in a new way of celebrating Holy Cross Day at my former parish in upstate New York, showed the same. I can also testify that developing the habit of looking for *viriditas* has made me more aware of it. No longer is a visit to a beautiful garden, or a walk through a fragrant woodland, merely an exercise in nature appreciation. I look for something more, stretching out my soul's antennae for the subtle breath of the Spirit cocreating amid the greening, and often feel it. Music is different for me now too, especially group singing: joyful voices raised together truly are an opening to life itself.[174] Slowly then I have come to trust that New Creation is not only a principle, it is a living presence, and having found it to be so, now I wonder why I ignored it for so long. For what it is worth, my personal experience is that "Paradise-based" living can definitely hold one's interest. It is in its own gentle way a demonstration of Spirit and of power.

I would add that several vignettes mentioned in the preceding pages have become touchstones for me out of the vast history of the Christian community. Let me list a few that stand out in this way:

---

174. I must mention with gratitude the constant and unselfconscious singing of the students at the Facultes de Science Infermiere et Rehabilitacion de Leogane in Haiti. During my year in their company, I marveled hundreds of times at how natural song can be. The men's dormitory was a paradise of music both day and night.

- Evangelism, particularly in Armenia and northern Europe. In Armenia, "Priests began to speak of the cross as an all-bearing tree sheltering the whole earth, or as a winepress on which divine grapes were pressed. . . . The combination of old and new symbols appeared enticingly alive and inviting"[175] (chapter two). In northern Europe, thanks to the efforts of wandering Anglo-Irish missionaries, "The promise of salvation and Paradise was the central message of the Christian church for the pagan peoples"[176] (chapter five). These powerful examples surely are worth trying afresh.
- Catechesis, and the baptismal preparation of ancient times. "A very early source, *The Odes of Solomon*, "defines baptism as being taken back to paradise, the land of eternal life, where blooming and fruit-bearing trees are irrigated by rivers of gladness"[177] (chapter one). How helpful it would be to understand preparation for incorporation in the Christian community in this evocative manner.
- Hildegard's use of "life itself" as the canon of theology. "Hildegard develops her thought from organic concepts like "life" and "greenness" or "viridity." This is by contrast with other medieval theologians such as Anselm who "takes for granted the capacity of reason to come to terms with static philosophical concepts like 'being,' 'substance,' and 'accident'"[178] (chapter five). We live in days that certainly prefer organic concepts to static ones.
- Ruthwell's runes and vine-scrolls. "The upward and downward motions belong together: they form a unity. It was the poignant dying of Jesus that won for us the new creation, a re-opened Paradise of eucharistic sharing represented by the symbol of the True Vine" (chapter one). Tracing these intertwined motions with the eyes and the heart is a meditation that never grows old.

175. Petrosyan, "The Khachkar or Cross-Stone," 62.
176. Wamers, "Insular Art in Carolingian Europe," 38.
177. Jensen, *Baptismal Imagery in Early Christianity*, 183.
178. Mews, "Religious Thinker," 56–57.

- Halevi's two symbols of life out of death in cases of modern genocide: "A large stone cross: a *khatchkar,* the ancient Armenian cross
  of resurrection, whose extremities ended in flowers, resembling
  a tree in bloom. It was a beautiful cross. And it reminded me of
  the logo I'd seen of a Holocaust survivor organization: a row of
  barbed wire sprouting into a bud"[179] (chapter six). It is so helpful
  to have a form of the Cross that invites community across lines of
  division.
- Disibod, who was himself "the greening finger of God" (chapter
  five). Perhaps each of us has a similar power of bringing life, if the
  virditas of the Spirit can flow freely.

These episodes from our collective past help me believe that there really
is something to it, that the Tree of Life can indeed be trusted to be a
source of rejuvenation and the fruits of the Spirit, now as it was in the
beginning. Thus, emboldened by my own experience and that of the
ages, I invite others to share the task of cultivating this Tree, amid the
garden which God plants for us today.

Epilogue

Mary Magdalene, apostle to the Apostles, was the first to know of the
resurrection. She met Jesus in a garden, where he stood before her, full
of life. She wished to cling to him but he would not allow it, saying, "I
have not yet ascended to my Father." In due course Jesus did return to
God, but he did not leave us comfortless. He sent the Spirit, and also, it
would seem, he gave us a symbol to stand for him in all his gracious presence while this age shall last. The Cross itself is a gift, for it represents the
whole mystery of Christ. Among the myriad forms this simple shape has
taken, Mary would, I suspect, especially appreciate the Cross depicted
as the Tree of Life. It would remind her how green the garden was when
Easter's dawn showed the Risen One alive, and giving life.

---

179. Halevi, *At the Entrance to the Garden of Eden,* 154.

Going Deeper

- How do you feel about the fact that to many non-Christians our primary symbol represents terror or oppression? Do you agree that images of the Cross as Life-Giving Tree are less apt to create such associations?
- A Holocaust survivor organization uses barbed wire sprouting into a bud as its logo. Is this the same as the symbol of a Life-Giving Tree or different?
- How might you share in the task of cultivating the Tree of Life in our own times?
- Do you think the garden in which Mary Magdalene met Jesus on Easter Day really might have been especially fragrant, and beautiful—a renewed creation?

Bibliography

Works Cited in the Text

Bitton-Askelony, Brouria. *Encountering the Sacred: The Debate on Christian Pilgrimage in Late Antiquity.* Berkeley: University of California Press, 2005.

Brock, Rita Nakashima, and Rebecca Ann Parker. *Saving Paradise: How Christianity Traded Love of This World for Crucifixion and Empire.* Boston: Beacon Press, 2009.

Brown, Michelle. "The Eastwardness of Things: Relationships between the Christian Cultures of the Middle East and the Insular World." In *The Genesis of Books*, edited by Matthew Hussey and John Niles, 17–49. Turnhout: Brepols Publishers, 2011.

Brown, Peter. *The Rise of Western Christendom: Triumph and Diversity AD 200–1000.* Cambridge, MA: Blackwell, 1996.

Cassidy, Brendan. "The Later Life of the Ruthwell Cross." In Cassidy, *The Ruthwell Cross*, 3–34.

———. *The Ruthwell Cross: Papers from the Colloquium sponsored by the Index of Christian Art.* Princeton: Princeton University Press, 1992.

Caviness, Madeline. "Artist: 'To See, Hear, and Know All at Once.'" In Newman, *Voice of the Living Light,* 110–24.

De Beaufort, Joseph. *The Practice of the Presence of God.* Brewster, MA: Paraclete Press, 1985.

Dinwiddie, John Linton. *The Ruthwell Cross and Its Story: A Handbook for Tourists and Students.* Dumfries: Robert Dinwiddie, 1927.

Fassler, Margot. "Composer and Dramatist: 'Melodious Singing and the Freshness of Remorse.' " In Newman, *Voice of the Living Light,* 149–75.

Gauckler, Paul. *Basiliques Chrétiennes de Tunisie* (1892–1904). Paris : A Picard, 1913.

Glaze, Florence E. "Medical Writer: 'Behold the Human Creature.' " In Newman, *Voice of the Living Light*, 125–48.

Grabar, André. *Ampoules de terre sainte.* Paris: C. Klincksieck, 1958.

Grierson, Roderick. "Dreaming of Jerusalem." In Heldman and Munro-Hay, *African Zion: The Sacred Art of Ethiopia*, 5–17.

Halevi, Yossi K. *At the Entrance to the Garden of Eden: A Jew's Search for Hope with Christians and Muslims in the Holy Land.* New York: Harper Collins, 2002.

Hart, Columba, and Jane Bishop, trans. *Hildegard of Bingen: Scivias.* Mahwah, NJ: Paulist Press, 1990.

Heldman, Marilyn E. "The Heritage of Late Antiquity." In Heldman and Munro-Hay, *African Zion: The Sacred Art of Ethiopia*, 117–32.

Heldman, Marilyn E., and Stuart C. Munro-Hay. *African Zion: The Sacred Art of Ethiopia*, ed. Robert Grierson. New Haven, CT: Yale University Press, 1993.

Saint Hildegard of Bingen. *Symphonia: A Critical Edition of the "Symphonia Armonie Celestium Revelationum."* Translated by Barbara Newman. Ithaca, NY: Cornell University Press, 1988.

Horn, Walter. "On the Origin of the Celtic Cross: A New Interpretation." In *The Forgotten Hermitage of Skellig Michael*, edited by Walter William Horn, Jenny White Marshall, Grellan D. Rourke, Paddy O'Leary, and Lee Snodgrass, 89–98. Berkeley: University of California Press, 1990.

Horowitz, Deborah E. *Ethiopian Art: The Walters Art Museum.* Baltimore: Walters Museum, 2001.

Howlett, David. "Inscriptions and Design of the Ruthwell Cross." In Cassidy, *The Ruthwell Cross,* 71–94.

Irvine, Christopher. *The Cross and Creation in Liturgy and Art.* London: SPCK, 2013

Jenkins, Philip. *The Lost History of Christianity: The Thousand-Year Golden Age of the Church in the Middle East, Africa, and Asia—and How It Died.* New York: Harper Collins, 2008.

Jensen, Robin Margaret. *Baptismal Imagery in Early Christianity: Ritual, Visual, and Theological Dimensions.* Grand Rapids, MI: Baker Academic, 2012.

———. *The Cross: History, Art, and Controversy.* Cambridge, MA: Harvard Press, 2017.

———. *Understanding Early Christian Art.* New York: Routledge, 2000.

Jones, Cheslyn, Geoffrey Wainwright, Edward Yarnold, and Paul Bradshaw, eds. *The Study of Liturgy.* New York: Oxford University Press, 1992.

Karkov, Catherine E. *The Art of Anglo-Saxon England.* Woodbridge: Boydell Press, 2011.

Kelly, Dorothy. "The Relationships of the Crosses of Argyll: the Evidence of Form." In Spearman and Higgitt, *The Age of Migrating Ideas*, 219–29.

Kitzinger, Ernst. "Anglo-Saxon Vine-scroll Ornament," *Antiquity Volume X* (1936): 61–71.

Kloss, Jethro. *Back to Eden.* Twin Lakes, WI: Lotus Press, 1989.

Mango, Cyril. *The Art of the Byzantine Empire 312–1453.* Toronto: University of Toronto Press, 1986.

Mann, C. Griffith. "The Role of the Cross in Ethiopian Culture." In Horowitz, *Ethiopian Art*, 74-93.

Mercier, Jacques. "Ethiopian Art History." In Horowitz, *Ethiopian Art*, 44–73.

Mews, Constant. "Religious Thinker: 'A Frail Human Being' on Fiery Life," In Newman, *Voice of the Living Light*, 52–69.

Morris, Collin. *The Sepulchre of Christ and the Medieval West: From the Beginnings to 1600*. New York: Oxford University Press, 2005.

Munro-Hay, Stuart C. "Aksumite Coinage." In Heldman and Munro-Hay, *African Zion: The Sacred Art of Ethiopia*, 101–16.

———. *Ethiopia, the Unknown Land: A Cultural and Historical Guide*. New York: I. B. Tauris, 2002.

Murray, Mary Charles. "Artistic Idiom and Doctrinal Development." In *The Making of Orthodoxy: Essays in Honour of Henry Chadwick*, edited by Rowan Williams, 288–307. New York: Cambridge University Press, 1989.

Newman, Barbara. " 'Sibyl of the Rhine': Hildegard's Life and Times." In Newman, *Voice of the Living Light*, 1–29.

Newman, Barbara, ed. *Voice of the Living Light: Hildegard of Bingen and Her World*. Berkeley: University of California Press, 1998.

Noga-Banai, Galit, and Linda Safran. "Late Antique Silver Reliquary in Toronto." *Journal of Late Antiquity* 4, no. 1 (2011): 3–30.

Ó Carragáin, Éamonn. *Ritual and the Rood*. London: British Library, 2005.

O'Loughlin, Thomas. *Adomnan and the Holy Places*. London: T&T Clark, 2007.

O'Reilly, J. "The Trees of Eden in Medieval Iconography." In *A Walk in the Garden: Biblical, Iconographical, and Literary Images of Eden*, edited by Paul Morris and Deborah Sawyer, 167–204. Journal for the Study of the Old Testament Supplement Series 136. Sheffield, England: Sheffield Academic Press, 1992.

Petrosyan, Hamlet. "The Khachkar or Cross-Stone." In *Armenian Folk Arts, Culture, and Identity*, edited by Levon Abrahamian and Nancy Sweezy. Bloomington: Indiana University Press, 2001.

———. *Khachkar: Origins, Functions, Iconography, Semantics*. Yerevan: P'rint'info, 2008.

Raw, Barbara C. " 'The Dream of the Rood' and its Connections with Early Christian Art." Medium Ævum 39, no.3 (1970): 239–56.

Richardson, Hilary. *Observations on Christian Art in Early Ireland, Georgia and Armenia.* Dublin: Royal Irish Academy, 1987.

————. "Remarks on the Liturgical Fan, Flabellum or Rhipidion." In Spearman and Higgit, *The Age of Migrating Ideas*, 27–34.

Richardson, Hillary, and John Scarry. *An Introduction to Irish High Crosses.* Dublin: Mercier Press, 1990.

Rice, D. Talbot. "The Leaved Cross." *Byzantinoslavica* 11 (1950): 72–81.

Spearman, R. Michael, and John Higgitt. *The Age of Migrating Ideas: Early Medieval Art in Northern Britain and Ireland.* Dover, NH: National Museums of Scotland, 1993.

Stack, Lotus. *A Christian Cross: A Woven Representation at the Minneapolis Institute of Arts.* Lyons: Centre International d'etude des textiles anciens, 1984.

Sweet, Victoria. *God's Hotel: A Doctor, a Hospital, and a Pilgrimage to the Heart of Medicine.* New York: Riverhead, 2012.

Van Engen, John. "Abbess: 'Mother and Teacher.'" In Newman, *Voice of the Living Light*, 29–51.

Van Tongeren, Louis. *Exaltation of the Holy Cross: Toward the Origins of the Feast of the Cross and the Meaning of the Cross in Early Medieval Liturgy.* Leuven: Peeters, 2000.

————. "Imagining the Cross on Good Friday: Rubric, Ritual and Relic in Early Medieval Roman, Gallican and Hispanic Liturgical Traditions." In *Envisioning Christ on the Cross: Ireland and the early Medieval West,* edited by Richard Hawtree, Juliet Mullins, and Jenifer Ni Ghradaigh. Dublin: Four Courts Press, 2013.

Vikan, Gary. *Byzantine Pilgrimage Art.* Dumbarton Oaks: Washington, DC: 1982.

Walsh, Peter G., and Christopher Husch. *One Hundred Latin Hymns: Ambrose to Aquinas.* Cambridge, MA: Harvard University Press, 2012.

Wamers, Egon. "Insular Art in Carolingian Europe: The Reception of Old Ideas in a New Empire." In Spearman and Higgitt, *The Age of Migrating Ideas,* 219–29.

Wendebourg, Dorothy. "Chalcedon in Ecumenical Discourse." Translated by Byron Stuhlman and Beth Schlegel. *Pro Ecclesia* 7 (1998): 307–22.

Wilkinson, John. *Egeria's Travels to the Holy Land*. Jerusalem: Ariel, 1981.

———. *Jerusalem Pilgrims before the Crusades*. Warminster: Aris and Phillips, 2002.

Liturgical Texts Cited

Book of Common Prayer. New York: Church Hymnal Corporation, 1979.

Exaltation of the Holy Cross: Processional and Adoration According to the Rite of the Armenian Church. New York: St. Vartan Press, 2007.

Festal Menaion. South Canaan, PA: St. Tikhon's Seminary Press, 1998.

The Roman Missal, Study Edition. Collegeville, MN: Liturgical Press, 2011.

Other Recommended Reading

Aulén, Gustav. *Christus Victor: A Historical Study of the Three Types of the Idea of Atonement*. New York: Macmillan, 1951.

Chazelle, Celia. *The Crucified God in the Carolingian Era*. New York: Cambridge University Press, 2001.

Corrigan, Kathleen. "Text and Image on an Icon of the Crucifixion at Mount Sinai." In *The Sacred Image East and West,* edited by Robert Ousterhout and Leslie Brubaker, 45–62. Urbana: University of Illinois, 1995.

Dalrymple, William. *From the Holy Mountain: A Journey Among the Christians of the Middle East*. New York: Henry Holt, 1998.

Dalton, O. M. *East Christian Art: A Survey of the Monuments*. Oxford: Clarendon Press, 1925.

Frolow, A. *La Relique de la Vraie Croix*. Paris: Institut français d'études byzantines, 1961.

Fulton, Rachel. *From Judgment to Passion, Devotion to Christ and the Virgin Mary, 800–1200*. New York: Columbia University Press, 2002.

Harbison, Peter. *The Crucifixion in Irish Art.* Harrisburg, PA: Morehouse Publishing, 1999.

———. *The High Crosses of Ireland: An Iconographical and Photographic Survey.* Bonn: R. Habelt, 1992.

Harries, Richard. *The Passion in Art.* Burlington, VT: Ashgate Publishing, 2004.

James, E. O. *The Tree of Life: An Archaeological Study.* Leiden: Brill, 1966.

Karkov, Catherine E., Sarah Larratt Keefer, and Karen Louise Jolly, eds. *The Place of the Cross in Anglo-Saxon England.* Rochester, NY: Boydell Press, 2006.

Karkov, Catherine E., and Robert T. Farrell, and Michael Ryan. *The Insular Tradition.* Albany: State University of New York Press, 1997.

Kitzinger, E. "A Pair of Silver Book Covers in the Sion Treasure." In *Gatherings in Honor of Dorothy E. Miner,* edited by Ursula E. McCracken, Lilian M. C. Randall, and Richard H. Randall Jr., 3–17. Baltimore: Walters Art Gallery, 1974

———. "Interlace and Icon: Form and Function in Early Insular Art." In Spearman and Higgitt, *The Age of Migrating Ideas,* 1–15.

Reijners, G. Q. *The Terminology of the Holy Cross in Early Christian Literature: As Based upon Old Testament Typology.* Nijmegan: Dekker & Van de Vegt, 1965.

Taylor, Joan E. *Christians and the Holy Places.* New York: Oxford University Press, 1993.

Underwood, P. A. "The Fountain of Life in Manuscripts of the Gospels." *Dumbarton Oaks Papers* 5 (1950): 43–138.

Werner, M. "On the Origin of the Form of the High Cross." *International Center of Medieval Art Journal* 29, no. 1 (1990): 98–110.